Industry leaders praise
How to Find and Cultivate Customers Through Direct Marketing

I totally recommend this book to anyone who is serious about direct marketing and recognizes the value of an individual customer. Martin Baier's book presents a superb business case for any company to create customers, but more importantly to cultivate them. Direct marketing has always been driven by statistics and finance. There is no one better than Baier, a master teacher, to explain how the numbers and finance work in direct marketing.

The added strength of this book is the case studies in each section which highlight the key principles of direct marketing and bring this to life.

Derek Holder
Managing Director
Institute of Direct Marketing

Martin Baier is a leader in the area of direct marketing, and now he's written a thorough guide in which he shares his vast experience and expertise. He has created a complete reference source for businesses dedicated to cultivating, keeping, and profiting from their customers.

John P. McMeel
President
Universal Press Syndicate

This "how-to" book provides a simple and readable approach to a complex discipline. Databases are demystified. Testing becomes a powerful weapon for market expansion. Analysis, segmentation and lifetime value are guideposts to employ for marketing success.

Martin Baier has written a thoughtful, practical compendium that demonstrates how the tools and techniques of direct marketing can be integrated to establish and maintain profitable relationships with customers.

Learn from one of the true masters of direct marketing!

Regina Brady
Director, Interactive Marketing
CompuServe

At last! Someone succinctly defines marketing theory and then brings it to life by using real-world examples of how that theory gets properly executed. By picking the most essential elements necessary to mine a customer database, Baier has taken a complicated subject and written a quick-reading, no-nonsense, direct-marketing cookbook. Who else could make multivariate analysis and relational database a good read?

Martin Baier is universally known for his direct-marketing skills as well as his academic expertise. Now he combines 50 years of direct marketing knowledge honed in the business world with over 25 years of classroom experience into one succinct, easy-to-read book. Whether you are a pro or a novice, if you really care about getting and keeping customers, this book is a must!

Greg Bruner
Vice-President
Montgomery Ward Life Insurance

Martin Baier's *How to Find and Cultivate Customers Through Direct Marketing* takes the newest and best direct-marketing concepts and shows you how to make them work in the day-to-day world of marketing. Whatever your field of marketing—manufacturing, retailing, cataloging, or fundraising—you will be exposed to insightful analyses that will help you build customer loyalty and profits for your company.

If you've ever wondered about such terms as regression and correlation analysis, list enhancements, enhanced PAR, lifetime value of a customer, or multivariate analysis, get this book. Baier talks about them in clear, easy-to-understand terms. He is at his best, demonstrating how techniques that originate in one marketing discipline apply to other areas of marketing, and the book is loaded with instructive case examples that show you how to apply these techniques. In other words, the theory comes alive at the point where it counts most . . . the bottom line.

The book, like the principles he lays out, is a win-win situation for any marketer—seasoned professional and newcomer alike.

Roland Kuniholm
Partner and Co-Founder
Frederiksen & Kuniholm

How to Find and Cultivate Customers Through Direct Marketing is a beautifully organized blueprint for the gathering and use of a database—stored customer information—as a strategic management tool. Baier's book is engrossing, but it is serious stuff. It took me just 4 1/2 hours to read, and I felt like I'd just been through an MBA Program in Direct Marketing.

Annie Hurlbut
President/CEO
The Peruvian Connection, Ltd.

A must read for anyone contemplating or just starting out in direct marketing. Even advanced and experienced direct marketers will learn from it. A lot of books cover mainly the "craft" or "how-to" side of direct marketing. Few discuss the theory—the why—of direct marketing. This book covers all the bases.

Written in an easy-to-read, easy-to-understand style and format, this book has got to be one of the better ever written on how direct marketing can be used and applied in virtually any situation.

Patrick Laughran
Director
Gestro Horne

Martin Baier constructs a practical, easy-to-use road map for effective marketing programs. Among other things, he shows you how to rationalize your marketing expenditures, target your field sales, and identify opportunities for high-impact community relations programs. Read this book and you'll begin to realize that it *is* possible to integrate the efforts of all your promotional tools.

Paul T. Allen
Director, Worldwide Cruise Marketing
Holland America Line

If you choose to read just one book on the subject of finding and keeping customers, this is it. It's unlikely that you'll find a more comprehensive easy-to-understand book on the subject.

Hermann Chan
Chief Executive
Times Direct Marketing Group
Founder, Asian Direct Marketing Symposium

Customers are the most important asset of a business, and Martin Baier has combined a wealth of personal experience and knowledge to write a must-read practical guide to customers.

The culmination of his professional achievements, Baier's newest book will become the most important item in your professional library. Keep it within easy reach. It will be referred to often.

William R. Denhard
Director of Sales
List Management Center
The McGraw-Hill Companies

In his relentless search for better ways to find and keep customers, Baier has built on a foundation of solid methodology and rigorous thinking, avoiding the quick fixes and cute slogans so prevalent in management thinking. For this reason, his contribution is lasting—the crowning achievement of his career-long leadership in the field of direct marketing.

William B. Eddy, Ph.D.
Dean and Harzfeld Professor of Management
Henry W. Bloch School of Business and Public
    Administration
University of Missouri—Kansas City

As a practitioner and an academic, Martin Baier has written a "must read" book for both audiences. He dwells with insight on the meaning of customer, ever mindful of the reader.

Richard L. Montesi
President
Direct Marketing Educational Foundation

I've been waiting for this book for a long time. Martin Baier's dedication to preaching the religion of directed, databased marketing has long been an inspiration to me and has impacted the entire direct marketing industry. With this insightful and fully comprehensive book, he has successfully captured the wisdom of his broad industry knowledge, summarizing all the important principles necessary for direct marketing success in decades to come.

Kurtis M. Ruf
Vice President
Ruf Corporation

Martin Baier's jargon-free book correctly details the essential elements of direct marketing with uncommon insight into the building of marketing databases, their use in affordably developing customers, and their value to an enterprise.

Henry R. "Pete" Hoke
Chairman of the Board
Hoke Communications

This book is like having an "expert program" at your beck and call to instantly serve up 50 years of priceless experience. Martin Baier is a whiz at making the complex easily digestible and showing just how valuable a customer can be made to be.

Stan Rapp
Chairman
Cross Rapp Associates

How to Find
and Cultivate
Customers
Through

DIRECT
MARKETING

How to Find and Cultivate Customers Through
DIRECT MARKETING

MARTIN BAIER

Foreword by Bob Stone

Printed on recyclable paper

NTC Business Books
a division of *NTC Publishing Group* • Lincolnwood, Illinois USA

Library of Congress Cataloging-in-Publication Data

Baier, Martin.
    How to find and cultivate customers through direct marketing /
Martin Baier.
        p.   cm.
    Includes bibliographical references and index.
    ISBN 0-8442-3666-7
    1. Direct marketing.   2. Database marketing.   3. Customer
relations.   I. Title.
HF5415.126.B336   1996
658.8'4—dc20   95–11296
                                                                 CIP

Published by NTC Business Books, a division of NTC Publishing Group
4255 West Touhy Avenue
Lincolnwood (Chicago), Illinois 60646–1975, U.S.A.
Manufactured in the United States of America.

5 6 7 8 9 0 QB 9 8 7 6 5 4 3 2 1

Dedicated to
Jonathan Baier Stein
and
Sarah Rachel Stein

Contents

PART IV
CUSTOMERS: HOW TO CREATE AND CULTIVATE THEM 177

PART V
CUSTOMERS: WHY TO CULTIVATE THEM 207

Foreword

"It doesn't show on your balance sheet, but your most valuable asset is your customer list."

So read the lead sentence of a sales letter first mailed in the 1950s by M.P. Brown, Inc. of Burlington, Iowa. The vice president and general manager of M.P. Brown, a firm that sold customer appreciation letters to businesses, was Martin Baier, author of this remarkable book.

The clarion calls of Martin Baier in all the decades that have followed the Burlington, Iowa, experience have been CUSTOMER recognition and appreciation and CUSTOMER cultivation. No one argues with the notion that it makes sense to nurture customers. That's a no-brainer. It's the "how-to" phase of building meaningful and profitable customer relationships that makes the difference.

Early on in his career, Baier learned that all customers are not created equal: historically 80 percent of repeat business comes from 20 percent of a customer base. Baier shows the way to targeting the best customer segments. And he takes all the mumbo jumbo out of defining technical advancements. The mysteries of regression and correlation analysis, discriminate analysis and cluster analysis melt away. Using his skills as master teacher, he walks us through case history after case history in the real world of building customer bases.

Baier is proof positive that you don't have to be a computer nerd to benefit from what the computer can do for you. He shows:

- How to build a database that includes the data you must have to maximize profits.

- How to apply the R/F/M formula so you can concentrate on the 20 percent of your customer base that brings you 80 percent of repeat business.

- How to determine the lifetime value of each customer in your database.

What Martin Baier says in this book focuses upon direct marketing principles, many of which he has invented, all of which he has refined and fine tuned. I feel it is important for me to emphasize that this book is in no way restricted to mail order. It is for *all business*, whether consumer or industrial. It is equally applicable for associations, service organizations, fundraisers, political organizations and retail store operations.

In short, you have in your hands a book just waiting to be mined by you. All of us buy some business books to scan, some books as reference sources. But I would put *How to Find and Cultivate Customers through Direct Marketing* into the ultimate category: I strongly recommend that you read this book from cover to cover. I think that by the time you finish the first chapter, you will opt for the total read-through.

Even if this book wasn't such an easy read, there would be a dominant financial reason to read on. The financial reason is that customers, cultivated properly, respond to offers at a rate of 400 to 800 percent greater than cold prospects.

Long live the CUSTOMER!

Bob Stone
Chairman Emeritus
Stone & Adler, Inc.

Introduction

I have been engaged in direct marketing all of my working life—so I have 50 years of experience. For half those years, I have taught direct marketing at the University of Missouri in Kansas City as well as around the world. That has added 25 years of academic expertise to my practical experience.

In *How to Find and Keep Customers through Direct Marketing*, I have put together those elements that my own experience and expertise—a combination that has worked well for me—have demonstrated that direct marketers need to know.

Drawn from a variety of areas, these essential elements of direct marketing are presented in this book in a logical sequence. They are brought together by a single word: *Customers!* This book is *about* customers. It is *for* those who want to understand and appreciate them.

Customers. *Which* organizations create and cultivate them? *Who* are they? *Where* are they? *How* do you create them? *Why* do you create them?

The five parts into which this book is organized deal in turn with the answers to these five questions. The parts evolve from the concept of direct marketing . . . to the development of a database . . . to research and testing . . . to creative techniques . . . to a view of customers as assets with a lifetime value.

Customers are the lifeblood of any organization. Whether an organization's customers are mail-order buyers, sales or service prospects, association members, fund-raising donors, political action supporters or retail store traffic . . . whether for-profit or nonprofit . . . whether consumer or industrial, customers must be the focal point of any successful direct marketing effort.

Thus, this book will be of interest and of value to business firms as well as not-for-profit organizations, private or public, large or small, dealing with tangible products or intangible services. It will have special relevance for those who take an entrepreneurial approach to their direct marketing efforts.

What This Book Will Do for You

- This book will guide you to learn more about and develop affinity relationships with your customers, so that you can cultivate them, even as you seek to create more like them . . . all through direct marketing.

- This book will teach you how to build a database, how to enhance that database in order to exactly suit your own needs, and how to profit from so doing.

- This book will enhance your understanding of market segmentation, consumer as well as business-to-business; it will show you how to segment markets to maximize your profits through increasing revenues and lowering costs.

- This book puts at your fingertips those techniques and tools of research and analysis about which you need to know so as to benefit from testing and experimentation.

- This book will integrate your thinking about your offers with that about your databases and with that about your promotions so that you can put them all together.

- This book will convince you of the importance of acquiring, keeping and growing customers . . . viewing them as assets with a lifetime value; diverting your thinking of promotion as an expense to its use as an investment directed to the creation and cultivation of customers.

For keeping me on this track and for helping me make complex subjects succinct and comprehensible, I am tremendously grateful to Anne Knudsen, the Executive Editor of NTC Business Books.

Here, then, is a comprehensive how-to guide, explaining how to use customer-focused direct marketing techniques to find, develop, retain and value long-term customers. An abundance of real-world examples illustrate subject matters, with case studies and workshops demonstrating key points. Proprietary data has been avoided in deference to the firms cited and so as to enable my own subjective judgments. Citations are from my own observations, not from factual interviews with individuals or organizations.

Martin Baier
Nellysford, Virginia

Customers: Creating and Cultivating Them

1

The Creation and Cultivation of Customers

Customers are the life-blood of *any* organization. Enterprise thrives on customers. They are the reason for its existence. This is because the primary purpose of any business, as well as any non-profit organization, is the creation and cultivation of customers. Without customers, organizations languish and die.

The customers these enterprises seek may be consumers, or they may be business buyers. Customers purchase products as well as services. They form affinities as members of groups, donors to charities, supporters of causes. They may even vote, whether in national political elections or in local forums.

Customers buy. They join. They give. They boost. They vote.

The creation and cultivation of customers is what this book is all about. *Who* are they? *Where* are they? *How* do you create them? *Why* do you cultivate them? *What* do you do to value them?

This book is concerned with a philosophy of marketing that has at its heart the needs, the desires, and the expectations of customers. It turns traditional views of business inside out by demonstrating that, instead of being in business to sell products or services, companies should be in business to *establish and maintain relationships with customers. Sales* are simply the result of such successful relationships.

As Peter F. Drucker has observed, "Companies are not in business to make things, but to make customers."[1]

---

[1] Peter F. Drucker, *The Practice of Management* (New York: Harper, 1959), p.37.

Customer Relationships and Affinity Marketing

Customers are not a homogeneous lot. Their one common characteristic is a relationship or affinity they form with those they favor with their custom—and often their continued loyalty.

When customers perpetuate such relationships, they expect in return to receive quality, value, service. Businesses, in turn, seek customer loyalty, in the hope of creating an affinity that will cement the relationship and keep customers coming back.

Relationships or affinities with customers can be developed to such a degree that loyal customers trust and buy the company's brands above all competitive offerings.

Often, even products or services outside the company's usual offerings and perhaps manufactured by an unrelated company, can, when offered to an "affinity group" of customers under the company's own brand, garner response much greater than if the same offer came directly from the "unknown" unrelated manufacturer.

Products as diverse as insurance and automobiles have long been sold successfully to affinity groups such as credit union members. Oil companies, department stores, and credit card companies all sell a great variety of unrelated merchandise to customers with whom they enjoy a relationship.

Examples of affinity are abundant. Here is one in which a bank offers a credit card to the shareholders of a mutual fund with which it is affiliated:

"Dear Franklin Shareholder:

As a shareholder of the Franklin Group of Funds, you have been selected for an exclusive financial opportunity.

You are qualified to apply for our Franklin Gold Card™—a prestigious VISA® card that can save you money every time you use it. Consider these money-saving opportunities:"

Airlines are among the most active affinity marketers. Frequent Flyer programs, for example, offer bonus mileage points for any purchase charged to a selected credit card. In a partnership between TWA and Diners Club, frequent flyers are offered a free card as well as bonus miles:

> Dear TWA Frequent Flight Bonus Member:
>
> I'm writing to you today because I don't want you to miss this special opportunity to earn <u>extra TWA Frequent Flight Bonus miles.</u> And through this special arrangement between Diners Club and TWA, earning extra miles is so easy.
>
> Just apply today for the <u>Diner Club Card Free</u> of the annual fee for the first year. Then, when you become a Card member, you can enroll in Club Rewards and start earning valuable points.

Other successful affinity partnerships include a special insurance plan offer from Allstate Insurance Company to Sears' customers and a Seiko watch offered exclusively to members of the Daughters of the American Revolution.

Some companies use the power of affinity marketing to sell other merchandise under their own name. Eastman Kodak Company, which had claimed that its cameras were the world's largest user of batteries, now quite logically sells batteries under its valuable brand name. John Deere Company's mail-order catalog offers an array of consumer products far different from the farm machinery with which the Deere brand has long been associated.

Many brand names, trading on their affinity relationships with customers in the marketplace, have been licensed to unrelated organizations for use on their products and services.

Affinity and good customer relationships extend their value well beyond the first sale . . . to cross-selling of unrelated products/ services, even from unrelated organizations. The power of the marketing database makes all of this and more possible.

Success Story in Affinity Marketing
Gerber Keeps Customers from the Cradle to the Grave

Affinity marketing knows no limits. The value of keeping customers is well illustrated by Gerber Products, best known for its line of baby foods which, to use Gerber's own words, ". . . has been helping parents raise happy, healthy babies since 1928."

With a track record of success and a highly visible brand name and preference, it made good sense for Gerber Products to capitalize on its customer relationships and venture into other appropriate product lines.

An early experiment was the Gerber Life Insurance Company, which coined an appropriate slogan, "Ask your baby about us." Logically enough, the selected market segment was a readily available prospect database: young parents with newly born babies.

Parents were offered a low-priced term life insurance policy that automatically covered the baby for a very reasonable beginning premium rate. This rate was guaranteed until the child reached age 27. Upgrades of the initial amount of life insurance became available at certain renewal ages with an automatic conversion privilege to permanent life insurance at age 27.

While Gerber's basic line of baby foods was a grocery store staple, its life insurance was offered by mail order. Direct-mail advertising was benefit-oriented and dwelled on customer relationship even though there was available no customer list or database of those who had purchased Gerber baby food.

Continuity selling involved periodic renewal of the child's policy via the parents and coverage was offered, also, to additional children as they were born to these parents.

After age 27, cross-selling accelerated with offers now going directly to the young adult child. Copy was on the order of: "Your parents bought this life insurance for you when you were born and have been paying the premiums ever since. Isn't it time you started buying your own life insurance?" The slogan on the letterhead now read:

GERBER LIFE INSURANCE COMPANY

A separate subsidiary of Gerber Products,
the baby food people you have known
since you were an infant.

That's a *relationship*. That demonstrates an *affinity*. That's an example of *continuity*. That's the power of an on-going *database*. That's *benefit-oriented* response advertising.

But, wait. There's more. When a parent, whose child still had one of those "starter" policies still in force, became a grandparent, the direct-mail letter received *by the grandparent* from Gerber Life Insurance Company began:

> When your grandchild was born . . . you probably felt emotions only a grandparent can really feel and understand . . . a delight and wonder at the continuance of life, and a firm commitment to do all you can to secure the future happiness and safety of that tiny infant . . . .

One grandparent receiving such a solicitation knew all about the birth lists Gerber was using. But where, he asked Gerber's president, was the *database of new grandparents?* "I think you'll have to get that information from your daughter," the president replied, "since we have a number of programs running in conjunction with our parent and sister companies which develop names of potential customers for us . . . and we take it from there."

Gerber Life's "sister" company, it turned out, was Century Products, a manufacturer of baby furniture. The warranty card included with the baby bed the daughter had bought asked for the names of both sets of grandparents!

Never underestimate the potential of a database!

Customer Relationships and Customer Value

The creation of customers is only a first step in building a successful business. The next—and more important step—is to keep and cultivate these customers.

In the past, the nurturing of customer relationships has been difficult, in fact almost impossible to evaluate. Though businesses may have known that the number of customers increased or decreased, that advertising attracted some new customers or that competitors took away others, there were few ways of knowing *which* customers came or went or *why*. The bigger the business, the more difficult the measurement.

But database technology has changed all that. Through database technology, an organization can at last identify its loyal customers, its repeat purchasers, and its one-time-only "triers," especially within well-defined market segments. Moreover, marketers can now trace each customer's actions and transactions. This ability makes customers a very significant—and measurable—asset.

Customers have intrinsic *value* in that the first sale to a newly acquired customer is but a forerunner of additional future sales to that customer. Customers are, however, the most elusive of intangible assets an organization has. Their "goodwill"—the ability of the organization to keep them—is the source of future revenues and future profits, which can go well beyond recovering the initial high cost of attracting or acquiring them.

Edward C. Bursk makes this point clear when he notes, "a company's investment in customers can be just as real as its investment in plant and equipment, inventory, working capital, and so forth. And it can be even more valuable in dollars and cents."[2] Bursk goes on to point out that although organizations may invest heavily in new product planning or in promotion of brands, they are less likely to invest in an area that is even more central to decision making. Companies almost never capitalize on what could be their most important asset—their customers.

Mail-order firms, faced with high front-end printing and circulation costs, long ago adopted the concept of *lifetime value of a customer* (LTV) to guide marketing decision making.

Recently, some packaged-goods companies have also been slowly moving toward customer valuation. London-based Grand Metropolitan PLC, upon its acquisition of Pillsbury and the Pillsbury Doughboy, announced plans to show on its balance sheet a value for all its major brands: Green Giant vegetables, Häagen-Dazs ice cream and the brand Van de Kamp's.

A 1993 Supreme Court decision could hasten a more universal adoption of the LTV concept. The case involved a New Jersey newspaper that claimed depreciation deduction for its acquisition of a paid-subscriber customer list as part of a sale transaction. In its ruling, the Court rejected the categorical argument presented by the IRS that customer lists are a form of goodwill and therefore never depreciable. This means that, if companies can determine the dollar value and useful life of lists of readers, clients, or policyholders, they may seek federal tax deductions based on the depreciation of those intangible assets.

---

[2] Edward C. Bursk, "View Your Customers as Investments," *Harvard Business Review*, May–June 1966, pp. 91–99.

Direct Marketing
THE POWERHOUSE BEHIND AFFINITY MARKETING

The tool that makes affinity marketing possible is direct marketing. Direct marketing has its roots in mail-order. Long before the 1950s, when the concept of "marketing" first appeared on the business scene, mail-order firms were already using mailing lists of prospects and transaction data to create new customers and then to cultivate those they already had.

These entrepreneurs mailed highly specialized niche catalogs (Henry Field Seed & Nursery Co., L. L. Bean), solicited special-interest magazine subscriptions (*Time, New Yorker, Saturday Review of Literature*) and offered general merchandise (Ward's, Sears', Spiegel's) to lists of potential customers—and to prior customers, about whom they had *data*.

Today's direct marketing, though, is much more than simply a subsection of the marketing concept. It is a philosophy of enterprise, an attitude, a belief . . . *a way of running an organization.*

At its very core are customers. What makes direct marketing unique from traditional marketing is: it begins with information about customers and uses this *database* to build relationships.

There are two other very distinguishing characteristics. First, direct marketing is always *measurable and accountable*. Every direct marketing cost can be related to a result. Second, direct marketing emphasizes *customer benefits* over *product features*. Quite simply, instead of answering the question "what is this product?", direct marketing answers the question "what can this product do for me?"

The power of database technology ties these three characteristics together. The database collects and analyzes customer information; it provides the means for accurately measuring results; and it is uniquely able to target specific benefits to specific customers.

The key objectives of direct marketing are two-fold: to *create* customers and to *cultivate* customers. Whether for selling products or services through the mail, or by telephone, or for generating leads for business-to-business salespeople, or for stimulating retail store traffic, direct marketing works to acquire new customers, and then to cultivate them through continuity selling and cross-selling.

The database lies at the center of all direct marketing efforts. Basically, a database is a customer list to which has been added information about the characteristics and the transactions of these customers. Businesses use it to cultivate customers and to develop statistical profiles of prospects most like their present customers . . . as they seek new customers.

Where Did It All Begin?

There's nothing new about direct mail; it's as old as communications itself. The term "circular letter" has been attributed, facetiously, to the round clay tablets used in biblical times. And, history books record that the fires of liberty were stoked before the American Revolution by the Committee of Correspondence. Patriots such as John Hancock and Samuel Adams, dispersed as they were in colonial America, kept one another informed through a "circular letter."

Benjamin Franklin, later the first Postmaster General of the United States, published and mailed a book catalog of "near 600 volumes in most faculties and sciences" in 1744. The catalog of William Lucas, an English gardener, dates back to 1667. And, the first trade catalogs appeared in Europe during the mid-fifteenth century, soon after Gutenberg's invention of movable type.

From these early beginnings, there followed a proliferation of mail-order catalogs during the post-Civil War period when agrarian unrest, through the National Grange, fueled the popular slogan "eliminate the middleman." Then, as now, mail-order catalogs reflected social and economic change.

Beginning as books featuring seed and nursery products, mail-order catalogs of the late nineteenth century included sewing machines, dry goods, medicines, and musical instruments. Most firms were product specialists, and mail order was an alternative form of distribution.

In 1926 a milestone was reached with the founding of the Book-of-the-Month Club by Harry Sherman and Maxwell Sackheim. These veteran direct marketers noted how few bookstores there were relative to the large number of post offices capable of delivering direct mail and books economically and expeditiously. Doubleday Company launched a similar operation, the Literary Guild, in 1927. As time passed, over one-half of all hardcover books were being sold by mail-order methods.

Today, major retail book chains are utilizing the tools and techniques of these mail-order book sellers, notably the customer list or database, to bring customers into their stores.

On the industrial scene, too, direct marketing has played an important role in the evolution of business-to-business distribution. The National Cash Register Company, as early as 1884, was probably the first to use direct mail to get qualified leads for follow-up by salespeople.

How Direct Marketing Works
THE SEARS STORY

There is a simple lesson to learn from the ups and downs of Sears Roebuck & Company: Stick to the principles that make direct marketing work. The Sears story, which began in 1886, demonstrates the dramatic growth of an entrepreneurial business into a giant organization which floundered when it strayed from many of the principles which it had literally invented!

The entrepreneur was Richard Warren Sears, a young railroad telegrapher in remote North Redwoods, Minnesota, who acquired a shipment of unclaimed and thus undeliverable gold-filled pocket watches, time-pieces of exceptional quality and accuracy.

Sears reasoned correctly that likely prospects and future customers for these fine watches would be railroad employees like himself. He just happened to have a "list" of 20,000 names and addresses, coupled with a *database* defining the railroad occupation of those on the list.

Sears offered his fine watches, by mail order, to specific *market segments*. Obviously, he approached other railroad telegraphers before "testing" engineers, conductors, or station agents.

He quite likely utilized a classic form of *direct-response advertising*, a letter with a reply device. The copy was probably pretty basic, but most certainly it carried a *benefit-oriented message* which may have read like this:

> Hey, I'm a telegrapher working for the railroad and so are you. I need an accurate timepiece and so do you. I just made an attractive purchase of unclaimed freight. And, I can personally vouch for the quality of these gold-filled watches. Do you want to buy one from me at a bargain price?

Legend states that Sears sold his watches in no time at all!

Was he way ahead of his time? You bet! Before long, his newly acquired *customers* were ordering *additional* watches. That probably prompted him to send another letter to those who had purchased a watch from him, suggesting they might need another one—an example of *continuity selling.*

Later, his *customers* began to send their disabled watches in for repair. That may have prompted yet another letter to his growing *database,* this one announcing that he was now in a new product line, the watch repair business—an example of *cross selling.* (Legend has it, too, that a watchmaker named Alvah Roebuck was eventually hired by Richard to help with the burgeoning repair business.)

By 1897, eleven years after his fortunate purchase and demonstration of *direct marketing* (although he certainly didn't call it that), Sears's original offer had expanded to a mail-order catalog of more than 750 pages with 6,000 items. By 1902, the sales of Sears Roebuck & Company exceeded $50 million annually.

Another chapter in the Sears story was written during 1993, a year which witnessed the demise of the near-century-old "Big Book," the Sears Roebuck Catalog which had been a household word to so many for so long.

Similarly, Aaron Montgomery Ward's experiment with a single-sheet discount catalog, which had preceded Sears' by fourteen years in response to the price inflation following the Civil War, came to its end as a general merchandise catalog in 1985.

Six years later, Montgomery Ward chairman Bernard Brennan announced an expansion of its *specialty* catalog business: "This business should not be confused with the old, traditional general catalog (since) it emphasizes target marketing, direct-mail support and specialty merchandise." Brennan added that this new specialty catalog business would capitalize on the Montgomery Ward name, heritage, and affinity with its large customer database.

As the rising and falling fortunes of Sears and Ward so clearly demonstrate, creation of customers is only half of what direct marketing is all about. To make it work in the long term, direct marketing must encompass continuity selling and cross selling in order to cultivate the customers it has striven to create.

Direct Marketing Must Be Strategic

Strategic management has been defined as "the *process* through which managers assure the *long-term* adaptation of their firm to its *environment* (emphasis added.)[3] In this sense, direct marketing can itself be viewed as a strategy . . . as a way of doing business in today's changing environment.

The chart that follows compares the modern view of strategic, as opposed to operational, management:[4]

	OPERATIONAL	STRATEGIC
Focus:	Internal	External
Time:	Short-Term	Long-Term
Scope:	Narrow	Broad
Uncertainty:	Ignored	Accepted
Alternative:	Limited	Significant
Perspective:	Departmental	Integrated
Level:	Hierarchical	Participatory
Investment:	Projects	Strategies

Strategy can be considered as the most important of all business disciplines because it causes the executive to question the fundamental premises of the status quo. It also serves as a starting point for direct marketers seeking new directions.

---

[3] B. S. Chakravarthy, *Strategic Management Journal*, 1986.
[4] Philip P. Crossland, Associate Professor of Strategic Management, University of Missouri–Kansas City.

WORKSHOP

Turning Madame Tussaud's into a Strategy-Driven Direct Marketer

This workshop is inspired by a 30-minute video titled "The Marketing Mix" that featured the famed London wax museum, Madame Tussaud's. In this hypothetical case, let's apply the "SWOT" model of strategic planning (*S*trengths, *W*eaknesses, *O*pportunities, and *T*hreats) to develop a direct-marketing strategy that will revitalize Madame Tussaud's. A SWOT analysis should also help answer the question that so often plagues would-be direct marketers: *Where Do I Begin?*

The video, produced by the British Broadcasting Corporation, describes some of Madame Tussaud's marketing challenges. We will use that information and come up with a strategy for using *direct marketing* to solve some of these problems.

In the video, Madame Tussaud's marketing director makes statements like "no customers . . . no business" and "marketing is a philosophy . . . with the customer at the core." He refers to FMCG . . . "fast-moving consumer goods" (packaged goods). He says that he wants to know *why* visitors come to the museum and exactly *what happens* during the visit. How might direct marketing help him answer his questions?

Perhaps the marketing director should consider the *lifetime value of a customer (LTV)*. A well-known brand name certainly opens the door to unique continuity-selling and cross-selling opportunities:

Continuity-Selling Opportunities

- Repeat visits to Madame Tussaud's wax museum in London

- Additional visits to Madame Tussaud's wax museums located in other cities of the world

- Visits to other London tourist attractions operated by the management of Madame Tussaud's, such as Windsor Castle and the Queen Victoria exhibit adjoining it

- Referrals to others by more than 3,000,000 annual visitors to Madame Tussaud's in London.

Cross-Selling Opportunities:

- Kodak products are already available in the museum: film, processing, stock slides, disposable cameras

- Why not a mail-order catalog offering artifacts, reproductions, related products appropriate for the image created by the Madame Tussaud's "experience?" The Metropolitan Museum of Art in New York City has run an extremely successful program like this.

Before Madame Tussaud's can consider launching benefit-oriented direct-response advertising, it needs to clarify its identity. What, really, *is* Madame Tussaud's? Is it a museum? Is it an entertainment? Is it an experience? Is it a tourist destination? Is it habit-forming, i.e., is there a potential for repeat visits by those on a database?

The marketing director also needs to consider the relevance and importance, if any, of a *database of customers*. A carefully constructed database might help Madame Tussaud's calculate the value of a customer; profile customers, by product and by source; cross-sell other tourist destinations or other products; or plan, forecast, and predict customer behavior. Is one called for here?

SWOT Analysis Findings

Here is a summary of strengths and weaknesses, based on information revealed in the Madame Tussaud's video.

STRENGTHS

200+ years of history
world-wide reputation
excellent location in the heart of London
good transportation links
close to other important attractions
(Planetarium, Baker Street, Regent's Park)
energetic, experienced marketing director
high-quality products
unique business

strong brand identity
enormous customer base
established relations with affinity suppliers
part of a bigger group
unlimited age appeal
appeals to all ethnic groups
enhanced fantasy
variety, with changing exhibits
interaction
technical skill of staff
price reasonable to tourist

WEAKNESSES

may still be perceived as old-fashioned
possibly a lack of agreement on corporate objectives
a specialized business with no clear product
definition: is it a museum, an entertainment, an experience?
no list of names, no database
limited capacity to value customers, to profile these customers
limited data in order to plan, forecast, predict, explain
continuity and cross-selling opportunities are also limited
each member of the Madame Tussaud's group independent of
      others
low repeat purchase
reliance on one-time tourist
queuing to get in, slow transaction
crowded
complex pricing
poor accessibility
perceived as dingy
little integration in promotions
relatively little promotion to locals
waxworks don't translate to reality
more topicality needed
long distances for cross-selling other attractions

It should be noted that strengths as well as weaknesses are *endogenous* to the organization. That is, they can be controlled from within.

Opportunities and threats, however, are *exogenous* to the organization and thus are not always easily controlled. Strengths can sometimes be used to exploit opportunities or to ward off threats. And, opportunities can sometimes be exploited to overcome weaknesses and thus ward off threats.

The opportunities and threats faced by Madame Tussaud's include the following.

OPPORTUNITIES

unlimited world market
opportunities for continuity selling
ditto for cross selling
opportunities to up-sell
opportunities to widen the product base
database opportunities for segmentation, profiling
opportunities in pricing through estimations of demand
   elasticities
price discrimination, e.g., premium prices, discounts
place opportunities, i.e., exhibitions to selected market segments
joint ventures with other of their own tourist attractions
increasing world-wide tourism
capitalize on topical changes
franchising
market/product differentiation
seasonal difference
using the ever-present queue (line) to cross sell
package sales to tours
cross sales of reproductions
exhibit wax likenesses of famous cartoon characters
direct-response advertising placed in remote locations
"Walkman" audio tours

THREATS

heavily reliant on tourists and thus . . . subject to exchange rates, terrorism, other exogenous factors

the "attractions" business in London is very competitive

domestic visitors see Madame Tussaud's as expensive

inflation and reduction in living standard . . . could further erode domestic business

degeneration of London and bad press

competitive tourist destinations

Identification of the Issues

The SWOT analysis clearly identifies Madame Tussaud's strengths, weaknesses, opportunities, and threats. From these we can next identify the *issues* of concern to the organization.

ISSUES

service industry with typical service delivery problems

smoothing demand (peak/off-peak)

database development . . . for promotion; for market research

customer acquisition

continuity selling . . . repeat visits

cross selling . . . within Madame Tussaud's; within the group

There are two means through which direct marketing can begin to address these issues: product management and promotion.

Product Management

New product development might suggest these starting points to encourage customer continuity, especially by London residents:

- Special exhibitions, such as cartoon characters
- Group sales
- Season tickets

- Off-peak hours events
- Referrals, bring-a-friend
- Exhibits in other London locations.

To enhance customer cross-selling opportunities, consider the following as starting points:

- Visits to other attractions in the London area affiliated with Madame Tussaud's
- Tie-ins with other local museums
- Mail-order catalog of reproductions of artifacts
- Videotapes and audiocassettes sales
- Adding value to the visit . . . developing a unique selling proposition (USP) for special groups.

Review of pricing strategy might be another starting point:

- Admission prices: individual, senior citizen, student, children, family, other "groups," season (high/low), overseas purchase, advance purchase
- Coupon tie-in with other product sales
- Premiums
- Gift book.

Promotion

In considering any promotion campaign, the direct marketer must live by these three rules.

1. Promotion must be measurable and accountable—where every cost is related to a result, often in the long-run (lifetime value of a customer).

2. Advertising must be benefit-oriented—it must tell prospects exactly what need or desire the product offered will satisfy.

3. Promotion must use and build upon real information about customers to support decisions, to identify prospects, to acquire, and then to cultivate customers.

A major advertising medium for Madame Tussaud's, as demonstrated in the videotape, was television. The commercials were exceptionally well done and certainly conveyed a compelling image of the wax museum as an "experience." Measurement of these, however, could be difficult.

Limited attention was paid to either direct-response offers or other media. An exception was the "leaflets" (so called by the marketing director) which were distributed in hotels and other tourist spots in the United Kingdom and in other countries.

Do these leaflets present the seed for a customer-oriented promotion? How about expanding distribution of these, with a response device added, to niche markets . . . to affinity groups . . . or through wholesalers such as travel agents, airlines, hotels, car rentals, credit cards?

How about testing and integrating the media and techniques of direct marketing with current promotion efforts? There's no need to *replace* promotion strategy at the outset. Rather, *augment* it! New offers. New media. Niches. Timing. Increased coverage. Increased market penetration.

The Need for a Database

A *database* is, of course, important. Although Madame Tussaud's marketing director admits to 3,000,000 visitors a year, there is no indication that any segment of these customer names or transactions or other characteristics has been captured, analyzed, utilized.

Why record visitors? It is, after all, highly unlikely that direct-mail promotion of another visit could pay for itself.

But . . . research of these names in their entirety (not just a small survey sample) could pay. Prospects could be identified for niche market promotion in media other than more-costly (per prospect) direct mail. Further, those who already have a customer relationship with Madame Tussaud's could be cultivated through mail-order cross selling of reproductions of artifacts and even vicarious visits through books, video and/or audio cassettes, or a printed publication to subscribers.

The *database* provides the means of research to support decisions. It enables profiling of customers so as to direct the search among prospects for more like them. It provides the means for implementation of profitable programs of continuity selling and cross selling. It aids scientific planning and forecasting.

When all is said and done, thinking like a direct marketer provides alternatives to the price competition which plagues so many in the tourism industry. *Non-price competition* is enhanced when offers and benefits are related to needs. It is enhanced, too, by database. And, by relating costs to results.

The Bottom Line

This case study suggests that direct marketing should not be viewed as an *alternative*. Rather, the tools and techniques inherent to the discipline can and should be *integrated* with existing strategy. *Direct marketing is itself a strategy!*

2

How Any Enterprise Can Use Direct Marketing

The tools and techniques of direct marketing can be used effectively by any *enterprise* for any response *transaction* at any *location* and at any *time,* regardless of *price.*

Direct marketing is, after all, simply a way of doing business. Whether an organization sells to consumers or industries, is for-profit or not-for-profit, or offers products or services, it can use direct marketing to create and cultivate customers.

These customers can be anywhere—and they are *everywhere.*

Census statistics that tabulate business activity refer to "location" of a sales transaction. These tabulations broadly categorize such transactions as:

- Those that occur at the *seller's* location;

- Those that occur at the *buyer's* location;

- Those that take place at a *remote* location, i.e., mail order;

- Those that occur through vending machines.

Most consumer transactions occur at the seller's location, typically a buyer visiting a retail store. Most industrial (business-to-business) transactions occur at the buyer's location, typically a salesperson visiting a firm. Remote transactions do not always involve the mail but may utilize the telephone and other interactive electronic media rather than a personal visit. Vending machines, accounting for a relatively small percentage of all transactions, are usually found in a variety of locations whose common characteristic is high traffic.

This chapter will demonstrate how the tools and techniques of direct marketing are being used to create and cultivate customers *at any location:* traffic-building at the seller's location; lead generation at the buyer's location; mail order from/to a remote location. It will look, too, at how some organizations are combining these locations in multi-channel marketing.

We will also show how direct marketing can apply to create and cultivate customers *in any situation:* product or service; consumer or industrial; for-profit or not-for-profit; fund raising; political action.

Building Traffic at the Seller's Location

Direct marketing's tools and techniques are playing a major role in boosting traffic and increasing sales *at the sellers' location,* where most retailing still occurs and will continue to occur.

Retailers such as department and specialty stores have long utilized direct marketing in the form of sale or seasonal catalogs and statement inserts. Some, Bloomingdale's for example, have gone so far as to set up mail-order profit centers. Customers, especially those at some distance from stores, are offered the convenience of shopping by mail or by telephone for items featured in these promotions.

A lot of customers like to "shop" from retail store catalogs but prefer to "buy" in the store itself where they can see and feel the merchandise, get a proper fit, and take delivery.

Many retailers, seeing the proliferation of mail-order catalogs in recent years, especially at the holiday season, have mistakenly equated the term "direct marketing" with "mail order." They have tended to view the latter as an *alternative* to in-store sales, rather than as an *adjunct* that can create store traffic at the same time as it generates added direct sales through mail or phone orders.

Retailers have also realized that catalogs are a useful means of building a customer database, something they in the past had neglected. These retailers have turned their charge account lists into mailing lists, if only to insert promotional offers with billing statements.

But customers who shopped in the stores and paid cash typically didn't make it to these lists. Neither did customers who chose to use credit cards other than those issued by the store, until recent technology made capturing these transactions convenient.

In response, retailers began to institute often rather cumbersome procedures to capture cash customer names at the check-out register. One very workable system was that developed and still used by Radio Shack, the national chain of electronic product retail stores.

Today, customers who make a purchase in any Radio Shack are asked for the last four digits of their telephone number. A computer terminal at checkout lists all those in that store's database identified by these digits. The customer's own record, then, becomes the basis for printing the current sales ticket while the database itself is updated. Periodic direct mail, often sale circulars, promotes return visits by customers.

Some Interesting Techniques for Retail Traffic-Building

France Loisirs, a French book club unit of the German publishing group, Bertelsmann, has strategically located its retail bookstores by studying the geographical distribution of its book club members. A single retail location serves about 10,000 members. Admission to a store is by membership card only. Typical direct-mail catalogs announce current selections, which members (if they so choose) can purchase at their local limited-access store. To provide meaningful service on each customer's visit, store clerks can access a database of the individual customer's reading preferences and prior purchases.

While the French book club integrated its mail-order activities with retail stores, an American book store chain, WaldenBooks, built a database of several million of its own retail customers. It generates ongoing relationships by giving regular customers a membership card and discounts that encourage repeat visits and cross-selling.

A food store in McLean, VA, built traffic and upgraded the purchase amount by handing entering customers a packet of coupons to be used during the current store visit. There was even a mail-order offer, for stationery, included in the packet of in-store specials.

Another interesting example of retail traffic-building comes from the motion picture industry. Warner Brothers capitalized on its affiliation with publisher Time, Inc. in the formation of a new organization, Time Warner. To promote its World War II movie, "Memphis Belle," Warner Brothers called on the direct-marketing experts at its affiliate, Time Life Books. It then mailed 700,000 postcards offering a special $1 discount to each recipient and a guest on evening performances of the new movie. The recipients were purchasers of Time Life Books or videos on such subjects as World War II, Nazi Germany, and aviation—all likely to be interested in the movie.

Manufacturers, too, have utilized the tools and techniques of direct marketing to create retail traffic for their products. Many have built databases from warranty cards returned by recent purchasers of their products. Some, like Sony, have developed mail-order offers for accessories. Others have used warranties to build future retail-store traffic. Polaroid, introducing its Spectra camera, utilized such lists for ongoing communication with buyers. Mailings to buyers included discount offers, redeemable at dealers, for film, copies, enlargements, accessories, and video cassettes.

Retail Coupons for Packaged Goods

Couponing, a major form of direct-response advertising, has long been utilized to promote the sale of convenience goods in retail establishments. Such coupons have for the most part been mass-distributed through newspapers, magazines, and direct mail.

More recently, major packaged-goods manufacturers—among them Kraft Foods, RJR Nabisco, Quaker Oats, Philip Morris, Colgate Palmolive—have used redeemed coupons to develop databases of users in order to identify and build brand relationships. The effort has been costly, especially when related to typically low unit prices and short-term sales.

While a coupon offer for a low-calorie product, for example, might achieve 2 percent redemption from mass circulation in a newspaper, the redemption rate could climb *ten-fold* when mail is *directed* by a database to a market segment who are diet and weight conscious. But, the cost to reach that segment might multiply *twenty-fold!*

Still, the effort continues as packaged-goods firms target individuals with product offers relevant to them. Some are now thinking of the lifetime value of a brand-loyal customer rather than looking only at a single coupon redemption.

Measurement of Traffic-Building Promotions

Retailers often face the quandary of measuring the results of traffic-building direct-response advertising relative to its costs. There are a variety of ways to do this.

Dillard's Department Stores have mailed to customers a "Holiday Money Card" offering an extra line of credit until December 25th and not payable until February. Presentation of the personalized card makes it possible to identify and credit the promotion for the ensuing sale. Similarly, Dillard's and many others have distributed "Bonus Coupons" which, when redeemed, let the promotion's success be measured.

The Burberry Shop in London once offered a voucher for lifetime cleaning of a raincoat purchased that day. To claim the gift, the customer had to mention learning of the offer through a direct-response advertisement in that day's edition of *The London Times*.

Great Universal Stores (GUS), Burberry's parent organization and one of the leading retailing groups in Europe, rarely runs any advertisement, print or direct mail, without including the means for crediting the source of a mail-order response or a retail purchase.

The Marketing Vice President for a prominent furniture manufacturer lamented that it was difficult to measure sales attributable to millions of catalogs, some quite large and beautiful, which his firm distributed through dealers and Sunday newspapers. The firm was reluctant to stop distribution of such advertising because its dealers "counted on it," even though it could not attribute sales directly to these promotion pieces. The solution was to include a rebate coupon in each catalog, to be validated by the dealer upon an appropriate purchase and then sent to the manufacturer for redemption.

An intriguing traffic-building ad for The Custom Shop Shirtmakers began, "IF YOU SOMETIMES UNBUTTON YOUR COLLAR AT THE OFFICE, WE SUGGEST YOU READ ON." The ad explained that only a custom-made shirt provides "the extra quarter-inch you can't buy ready-made." "Think of this," the ad concluded, inviting the recipient to come to their store, "once we have your pattern, you can reorder by mail or phone—very convenient."

Another traffic-building offer appeared in a newspaper advertisement by The Martin City Melodrama and Vaudeville Co. It included a coupon proclaiming "$1 Off With This Ad!"

Who says you can't measure . . . even newspaper ads?

Devoted direct marketers sometimes feel sorry for those department stores, some quite large, who daily run page after page of newspaper advertising for bedding and clothing and the like. When asked if advertising pays, they don't really know!

Wasn't it the eminent department store retailer, John Wanamaker, who said, "Half of my advertising is wasted, but I don't know which half?" The direct marketer, who creates and then cultivates customers in a manner where results justify costs, *knows!*

Lead Generation at the Buyer's Location

The tools and techniques of business-to-business direct marketing date back at least half-a-century. John H. Patterson, who founded the National Cash Register Company (the forerunner of today's NCR), was probably the first to use direct mail to get qualified leads for his sales people to pursue. Patterson's lead generation efforts and his sales force follow-up were both directed to specific kinds of businesses that were likely to purchase his products.

The basic method of prospect qualification, augmented by direct-response advertising in a variety of media, still plays a big role in business-to-business marketing. As the cost of a personal industrial sales call has exceeded $250, with three or more calls the norm for converting prospects to customers, sales-lead generation has become commonplace.

No longer are leads generated through direct mail alone. All media are used now: print (newspapers, magazines); broadcast (television, radio); and most certainly the telephone. And while most lead generation is business-to-business, major consumer purchases such as home improvements or insurance may also entail lead generation.

In this section we will concentrate on lead generation for business-to-business sales at the *buyer's location*, since that is where major direct marketing growth has occurred in recent years. A consumer would likely go to the seller's location to replenish a supply of dry cell batteries. But in the case of an industrial purchaser seeking to acquire a power generator, the manufacturer would likely come to the buyer's location . . . *after* qualifying that buyer as a prospect.

A Case in Point: A Manufacturer of Corporate Aircraft

A well-known manufacturer of corporate aircraft is known to have developed a state-of-the-art database of key prospects for its high-cost products. It has used this database to generate highly qualified leads for follow-up by its dealers, who were involved in the process every step of the way.

The database itself was a composite derived and enhanced from many independent sources. It identified key characteristics of each prospect organization such as industry, size, length-of-time in business, number of employees, sales revenues, and other relevant factors. It also identified by name and title key decision-makers along with their addresses and telephone numbers.

Matching this file to a variety of other data sources provided key information about aircraft ownership, such as the manufacturer of and the type of aircraft, its age, as well as prior (but not current) ownership of aircraft.

The manufacturer's own database was scanned, and mail/telephone surveys authenticated and augmented this information. Dealers were called in to verify facts of the compilation. Each dealer then ended up with a comprehensive notebook containing a full page of information to qualify each prospect.

The direct mail sent to generate meaningful leads on behalf of the dealers was itself a textbook model. Benefit-oriented direct-response copy addressed the interests of the individual recipient, be that the Chief Executive Officer, the Chief Pilot, or the Chief Financial Officer. Relevant in copy, too, was whether the organization now owned the manufacturer's or a competitor's aircraft or none at all or none at this time.

The bottom line was, you guessed it, *success!*

Another Case Example: A Group of Soft-Drink Bottlers

Soft-drink bottlers have made their products conveniently available through vending machines located in high-traffic locations such as industrial plants, offices, hospitals, hotels, airports, bus terminals, and educational institutions.

Typically, salespeople representing bottlers have selected prospects from lists coded by standard industrial classification (SIC) and then visited them personally. A group of bottlers in New England discovered that it was closing only one sale out of ten calls by using this procedure. (At the McGraw Hill estimate of $250 per contact, and three calls, that comes to $7,500 to make one sale!)

Striving for efficiency, the soft-drink bottlers turned to direct marketing. Using basically the same SIC-coded prospect list, they sought to generate leads through direct mail.

But they went beyond simply name/address. How many employees were there in each plant or office? How many rooms in the hotel? How many students at the university? How many beds in the hospital? How many passengers in and out of the airport?

Further, how strong was their competition in each locale? What brands were preferred? How high did heat and humidity go?

All of these factors had a bearing on how many vending machines were needed at a location and the resulting size of the sale. Not only could the direct-mail copy address the benefits to be derived for a particular type of organization, but the salesperson could advise intelligently during a follow-up visit.

Bottom line, the New England soft-drink bottlers reported that the program generated one sale for every 3.7 contacts, at a cost-per-sale of $89. Better yet, 6.3 sales contacts were avoided, saving more than $250 a call!

As this case demonstrates, the only way you will ever know whether direct marketing "pays" is to measure results vs. costs.

Mail Order (and Telemarketing) To/From a Remote Location

Examples of remote location transactions through the use of mail order coupled with telemarketing are endless.

No longer is direct mail, including printed catalogs, the *only* medium. Printed media like newspapers and magazines are used extensively. So are broadcast media, television, and radio. Most recently, electronic media have arrived on the scene: interactive personal computer hookups, interactive cable TV, and telephone/television hookups, are all expanding the possibilities.

When it is commonplace to order an exercise machine demonstrated on TV via a toll-free "800" telephone connection, then have the product delivered by United Parcel Service, it is apparent why the term "mail order" has become an anachronism!

The Organizations That Use "Mail Order"

To begin with, mail order was truly to/from a remote location! General merchandise catalogs were geared to rural areas. Specialty magazines were of interest to small numbers of the total population who were widely dispersed. Benjamin Franklin's 1744 book catalog addressed itself "to those persons who live remote." Most offers, excluding the now-defunct general merchandise catalogs, were specialized.

Today, anything that can be sold, can be sold by mail or phone! But the special nature of the offer is paramount. A real estate broker is more likely to sell a castle in Ireland by catalog than a row house in Philadelphia.

Look at the catalogs and single item offers in your own mail and note how specialized they are. Magazines like *Newsweek, New Yorker, Smithsonian, Fortune,* and *Playboy.* Casual clothing from L.L. Bean, Lands' End, and Eddie Bauer. Alpaca products from the Andes Mountains via the Peruvian Connection catalog. Up-scale and even luxury goods from Neiman-Marcus. Specialty clothing from Ann Taylor and Talbot's.

Popcorn delicacies from Velvet Creme in Kansas. Original English Muffins from another Kansas firm, Wolferman's, a division of Sara Lee. Prime beef and gourmet foods from Omaha Steaks. Coffees from Gevalia Kaffe.

Kitchen products from Williams-Sonoma. And, garden products from its affiliate company, Gardener's Eden. Living plants from Breck's and a host of other seed and nursery catalogs, some more than fifty years old. Books and videos and compact disks galore. Newspapers and all kinds of magazines.

Limited application products, too, like those featured in ads in airline magazines and in the catalogs and stores of The Sharper Image. (An observer of one of these catalogs once commented, "Have you ever in your life seen so many things you can do without?")

Business books, like this one, from NTC. Office supplies and furniture products from Reliable, Quill, and others. There are computer offers by the dozens, hardware and software and the newest in technology. The list goes on, business *and* consumer.

Paramount to the success of mail order is a differentiated product appealing to a niche market. Important, too, is the promotion of that product. Not just any advertisement will do the job. The ad must be benefit oriented and it must be geared to eliciting a response. And *most* important is the list.

The power of database has been a major factor contributing to the ongoing success of the mail-order distribution system. That goes back to mailing lists, really, which have been a key stimulus to today's direct marketing. Especially interesting in this evolution, though, is the fact that we no longer look at mail order as an *alternative*. Rather, the tools and techniques of mail order have blended throughout our distribution systems, as we next demonstrate.

Multi-Channel Distribution

Browse major shopping malls in the United States and you will be surrounded by stores with such names as Williams-Sonoma, Talbot's, Laura Ashley, Sharper Image, Abercrombie & Fitch, Spencer Gifts, Hickory Farms, Lee Ward, Eddie Bauer, and Ann Taylor.

Each of these retail chains has its roots in a mail-order catalog. Every one of them understood in the beginning and still understands now the tools and techniques of direct marketing. Whether their sales are consummated from a remote location (mail order) or at the seller's location (retail store), the principles are the same.

A great deal of marketing synergy can be created between the catalog and the retail store. When Williams-Sonoma opens a new retail store, it prints an invitation to visit the new store on catalogs going to its mail-order customers in the area. Talbot's sends a discount coupon to encourage mail-order customers to shop in a new and conveniently located store.

While catalog companies have been opening retail stores, those already there have been building store traffic with specialty catalogs, especially to present CUSTOMERS!

Direct Marketing Works for Both Products and Services

Product and service enterprises alike use the techniques and tools of direct marketing to create and cultivate customers.

A notable and ongoing example of that statement is American Express, which has long been offering intangible services and tangible products through highly sophisticated database segmentation modeling and selection techniques.

American Express builds continuing customer relationships with offers to its credit cardholders of a variety of insurance (life, accident, health, credit card loss) and other financial services (investments, loans). It frequently offers as well a large variety of merchandise products, mostly travel related.

Cardholders are regularly encouraged to upgrade their status from Green to Gold to Platinum cards, each with its own set of service benefits. Upgrades are offered to life and health insurance. Automatic flight insurance is provided as well. So is nursing home insurance coverage. All the while, merchandise catalogs are sent to present customers to encourage them to buy more. Products are offered through billing inserts as well.

To top it off, American Express capitalizes further on its good customer relationships through discount and other promotion offers on behalf of its travel partners: restaurants, airlines, hotels, car rentals, cruise ships.

A large majority of customers who do business with stock brokers, it has been reported, *have never seen their stock brokers!* Many investor funds and discount brokerages seek and maintain customer relationships remotely, by mail or telephone or other interactive media such as CompuServe installed on personal computers. More and more travel itineraries are being handled remotely by mail order or by telephone contact resulting from direct-response advertising. Use of the telephone, of course, is not new to either stock brokers or travel agents.

And, when we consider the abundance of services now being offered in a targeted sense, we certainly shouldn't overlook the growth in response advertising by a variety of professions, including lawyers, accountants, engineers, and specialty medical practitioners. For example, consider the orthodontist seeking to offer his specialized dental services to families with young children or the ophthalmologist seeking to treat eye cataracts occurring in older patients.

A Special Product/Service Case: Personal Computers

Computer hardware and software, largely mainframe installations, have typically been offered by salespersons of manufacturers, notably IBM, calling at the buyer's location. While leads have been generated through direct response advertising in a variety of media, the "marketing representative" was—and remains—a key player.

But the PC—the personal computer—has paved the way for many innovative direct marketing applications.

Buyers of software for personal computers often register their purchases with the producers of operating systems and software applications, usually in order to access technical assistance and information about modifications or upgrades.

Thanks to this habit, software producers like Microsoft, WordPerfect, and Lotus have built extensive databases. Through information magazines, newsletters, and direct-mail solicitations, they are able to maintain ongoing relationships with their customers—and seize many opportunities for continuity selling and cross-selling.

The most frequent offers are for system upgrades and new applications. And because these customer databases have often been made available for noncompetitive offers—either by mail/telephone order or through resellers—customers can also purchase technical publications, continuous forms and stationery, entertainment, or utility software.

Hardware—the PCs themselves as well as their peripherals and accompanying software—is still largely distributed through dealer networks of retail stores. One manufacturer, Dell, has become a leader in both mail order and computer manufacturing. Dell and a host of mail-order price discounters have impacted the retail stores, taking sales but not necessarily service from them.

While IBM has experimented with "direct" off and on, only lately has it committed to it. So, too, have Apple and Compaq. Dell continues as a mail-order leader, but has also gone retail with distribution through Wal-Mart and Sam's Club.

The Microsoft Model of Direct Marketing

Microsoft, the leading manufacturer of operating systems for personal computers, provides an interesting example of the power of a database and the customer orientation it makes possible.

This example begins ten years ago with the purchase of a personal computer from a retail store, with Microsoft's MS-DOS® operating system installed. Soon after the reseller's customer registered that software, he received a letter from Microsoft's William Gates urging him to report uses of his disk operating system (DOS) for a newsletter to follow. That newsletter exchanged usage ideas and included information (with order forms) about new Microsoft products and tutorials. Ordering was *direct* and easy by credit card, through mail or "800" telephone service.

Direct-mail upgrades and new product cross-selling came regularly. While the customer could always choose to purchase from a retail store, the mailed offer came *direct to the user customer.* Contact accelerated upon the customer's installation and registration of Microsoft's Windows®. Direct mail then included catalogs of products suited for Windows®, from Microsoft as well as other software and supplies vendors.

The 1993 promotion announcing the MS-DOS® 6 upgrade arrived in the form of an "Upgrade Advisor" disk. "Run the Upgrade Advisor disk for a quick inventory of your system," the customer was instructed, "and a checklist of upgrades that make sense for you." Here was cross-selling in its finest hour, *based on what the customer had as well as what that customer might need.* Invasion of privacy? Not at all. What better way to be of potential service to a customer?

Following instructions for the disk resulted in a printout of a "Recommended Products List." Along the way, the customer was congratulated for already having installed the latest version of Windows®. When the printout noted the presence of Microsoft Excel® (spreadsheet) for Windows, but not Microsoft Word® (word processing) for Windows, the customer was offered a special price on the latter, together with a True Type Font Pack as a gift for replacing WordPerfect®.

What about "location"? The disk inventory repeatedly encouraged the customer to see a reseller for details. In fact, when the customer attempted to order the MS-DOS® 6 upgrade direct by phone, he was given three reasons why he would be better off visiting his reseller:

1. There would be immediate delivery from reseller stock with no shipping and handling charge;

2. Resellers were discounting the recommended list price;

3. The manufacturer's inventory was low and there would be a several-week shipping delay.

The customer ordered direct by telephone anyway because his nearest Microsoft reseller, who was indeed discounting the product, was 35 miles away. He waited six weeks for delivery!

Besides being a great example of location synergy, this Microsoft case study is an impressive example of ongoing direct marketing communication, geared to an individual customer's own PC usage needs, that takes lucrative advantage of a carefully structured database and offer.

Direct Marketing Works for Both Consumer and Industrial Goods

Consumer goods are now distributed using the tools and techniques of direct marketing, both at retail and remote (mail-order) locations.

As we have already demonstrated, packaged goods companies are using database technology to harness the power of coupons. Whether coupons are mailed, inserted in newspapers, or distributed at the point-of-purchase, database technology is helping these companies to define, segment and target markets.

Simultaneously, there has been much growth in business-to-business applications like those given earlier in this chapter: office products, computers and supplies, soft-drink vending machines, . . . even corporate aircraft.

But, how does a manufacturer of earth-moving equipment or heavy industrial cranes use direct marketing to find prospects? The principles for creating and cultivating industrial customers are the same ones applied in consumer markets.

The manufacturer of a highly specialized form system for heavy-duty concrete construction estimated that there were no more than a few hundred prospects for his product *world wide.* Demonstration was a powerful sales tool, but it required lots of travel and time. So he produced a video of several demonstrations and successfully offered it to a carefully compiled database of prospects.

A similar experience involved the manufacturer of the type of crane, large and cumbersome, which tall buildings are now built around. "How do you find and maintain contact with prospects?" this manufacturer was asked. The reply: "We regularly compile prospect lists from news and trade press reports. We write letters. We telephone. After qualification, there is appropriate personal follow-up."

It's no wonder that industrial mail-order and lead-generation programs are now possibly the fastest-growing segment of direct marketing.

Direct Marketing Works for Non-Profit Organizations, Too

Whether an organization is for-profit or not-for-profit, the tools and techniques still apply.

For many years tax refund checks issued by the Internal Revenue Service have been accompanied by mail-order forms for U.S. Liberty Coins from the U.S. Mint.

Educational institutions of many types have relied on the techniques of targeting to obtain enrollments, offer continuing education courses, raise funds, garner political support, and communicate with alumni and the larger community.

Much targeting goes on in health care, too. Medical specialists such as dentists and eye surgeons have long used direct marketing to reach their target markets. Hospitals, too, are increasingly turning to direct mail to market the expertise of their medical staffs. They set up fitness programs and offer them by direct mail. They invite, through direct-response advertising, those seeking special treatment, as for diabetic or heart conditions.

City Union Mission, at a time of dire financial need, put together a list of 4,000 prior contributors from whom they obtained donations totaling $350,000, with a single letter.

The Sisters of Mercy did likewise to raise funds for an addition to their nursing home. They, too, relied heavily on a story-telling letter, written by a nun who had majored in English Literature and had strong emotional ties to their activity.

Jerry Lewis raised a record $46,014,922 (plus $36,849,732 from corporate sponsors) to fight muscular dystrophy during his 21$\frac{1}{2}$ hour 1993 Labor Day Telethon.

The Korean War Veterans, seeking to build a memorial already authorized by Congress in the nation's capital, sought funds with an insert included in insurance premium billing sent by the Department of Veterans Affairs. The insert pointed out that "more than 20,000 contributed over $200,000 the first time a similar insert . . . was mailed."

Direct Marketing Works for Shaping Political Action

Political action groups also know about the techniques and tools of direct marketing. You'll see names in abundance in the membership roster of the Direct Marketing Association!

Do you want to be elected President of the United States? Mayor of your town? Governor of your state? A member of your school board? Try direct marketing.

Jake Ruf did when he became elected mayor of Olathe, Kansas. He relied on database market segmentation in his own sophisticated computer facility to identify the 30 percent of registered voters that would deliver 80 percent of the vote he needed to carry out his platform. He sent just two direct-mail pieces to just 12,000 of the town's 70,000 residents. He beat his rival by 30 percent in the primary; by 35 percent in the election. First time out!

For better or for worse, such organizations as the National Women's Political Caucus, People for the American Way, Citizens for Free Enterprise and the Physician's Committee for Quality Medical Care have been shaping public opinion with their direct-marketing efforts. So have organizations intent upon "saving" the Social Security and Medicare programs. And so have environmental groups like the Nature Conservancy, World Wildlife Fund, and Rails-to-Trails.

Then there are the numerous health-concerned organizations like the American Cancer Society, the American Heart Association, the American Diabetes Association, and the American Lung Association. All American, all supporting research for worthy causes—and all proponents of direct marketing to achieve their objectives.

A Concluding Word About the Relevance of Direct Marketing

The diverse applications presented in this chapter make abundantly clear the near-universality of the discipline of direct marketing for today's organizations. They make clear, too, that this way of doing business is not limited just to where its roots are: in a distribution system called mail order, and in an advertising medium called direct mail.

Remember, companies should be in business to *establish and maintain relationships with customers*. Sales are simply the result of such successful relationships. The tools and techniques of direct marketing—notably, a powerful database, an adherence to measurement and accountability, together with a benefit-oriented promotion—lead to the creation and then the cultivation of customers from whom relationships are derived.

Any enterprise can use direct marketing!

Directing the Location of a Sales Transaction[1]

This workshop is inspired by a situation in which a declining birth-rate has resulted in a declining market demand. These facts of life stimulated a British baby shoe manufacturer to develop a direct-marketing strategy that would influence buyer behavior toward its product line. The case workshop is presented here to stimulate your own thinking about this chapter's contents and applying such to your own situation.

Britain's largest shoe manufacturer, C&J Clarks, Ltd., faced a difficult sales problem. A declining birth rate in the United Kingdom caused a 13.1 percent decline in market demand for children's shoes.

As a result, retailers were carrying less stock and thus restricting consumer choice. Salespeople for C&J Clarks, Ltd., who called on some 2,000 retailers every 6 to 8 weeks, found it increasingly difficult to maintain retailer interest in carrying a full range of styles and colors, in spite of a schedule of magazine advertising that the firm was running in specialized media.

As an alternative to this general magazine advertising, executives of the firm decided to contact new mothers in another way and to measure specific results from that contact. The new promotional strategy involved use of The Bounty Box, a gift pack containing advertising and product samples, given to a new mother while she was still in the hospital. About 280,000 new mothers were reached through this medium every year, which was 80 percent of the potential market.

A mailing piece with a special offer was designed. The package contained a letter, a four-color brochure, and a reply card, low-key in nature and designed to position Clarks as a company that knows about babies. The letter offered a handsome color poster, 16 x 20 inches, which could be hung in the new infant's room at home. The poster depicted toy blocks, each containing copy describing "stepping stones" the infant would pass: crawling, sitting, speak-

---

[1] This case study is adapted from "British Shoe Manufacturer Builds Traffic for Retail Outlets," *Direct Marketing*, December 1978.

ing, standing, teething, and, of course, getting the first pair of shoes from Clarks.

This offer from Clarks, distributed within The Bounty Box, resulted in a 15 percent response requesting the poster. Clarks thus generated its own database of new mothers, about 42,000 annually. When it was time for the baby's first shoes, the mothers received a letter and a leaflet giving valuable guidance in buying the child's first shoes:

Dear Mrs. Jones:

During the next nine months or so your baby's going to start to walk. And although one of the healthiest things in the world is for him (her) to run around in bare feet, sooner or later he's (she's) going to need shoes.

Obviously, you're going to want good-looking shoes. But there are more serious considerations that should affect your choice. That's why we've sent you this leaflet explaining what you should be looking for in a child's first shoes and, more importantly, why you should take so much trouble over them.

When you've read the facts in the leaflet, we believe you'll decide to buy Clarks First Shoes. So at the bottom of this letter, we've listed your nearest First Shoes stockists.

Everyone of them has a trained fitter on the staff who'll be able to give you all the help you need in choosing the most important shoes you'll ever buy.

Yours Sincerely,

C&J Clarks, Ltd.

Not to leave a stone unturned, Clarks' salespeople presented to each retailer an outline of the program and a sample of The Bounty Box. They gave the retailer, too, a 5–by–7 inch bound presentation, printed on heavy paper stock. Each page described a typical fitting situation. The Clarks salespeople also left a window decal, a die-cut illustrating the baby's block idea, and, as an in-store display, a building block box stand on which to display their First Shoes.

It was suggested that the fitter ask for the name of the family making a purchase as a result of this program in order to contact them when the baby would be ready for another pair, another size.

The Bottom Line

What were the results? Against a declining market of 13.1 percent, Clarks First Shoes volume increased 4 percent. Retailers upped their stock orders 8 percent. After testing, the program became a continuing one.

The real learning experience here, however, may well be that of breaking with traditional ways of doing business, of seeking and experimenting with new and different ways of achieving results, relative to costs. The basis for such action is typically research and accumulation of facts.

In this case, generating store traffic for retailers may not have been the only solution. Can you think of others? What does the case tell you about creating and then cultivating customers? Can, indeed, *any enterprise* benefit from the tools and techniques of direct marketing? How about yours?

PART
II

Customers:
Who They Are

Creating and cultivating customers means knowing about your customers and their needs—so you can provide your customers with products and services that meet their needs.

The key to this knowledge is the database, the subject of the chapters in Part Two. We'll look at what a database can do . . . how to build it . . . what should be in it . . . and how to enhance it using information from outside sources. And we'll show you how to use the information captured in your database to construct a profile of your customers, and use it to find more just like them.

3

The Database:
The Key to Building
Customer Relationships

The database lies at the very core of marketing directed toward the creation and the cultivation of customers.

Once customers have been acquired, their actions need to be recorded so that each and every customer relationship can be cultivated.

Marketing databases can collect and manipulate information on customers, their individual characteristics and, most importantly, their response characteristics. With a database, marketers can use past actions by customers to predict their future preferences, or profile prospective customers for effective market segmentation.

In direct marketing, databases can describe environments in which a high propensity to respond (or not to respond) to an offer is likely. Customer databases can be enhanced with data from other sources so that they become even more descriptive of that environment. And, they can provide the basis for analysis, evaluation and scientific decision support which are key characteristics of direct marketing.

This information can add enormous value to customer relationships. Remember, keeping new customers is critical. Rarely will the cost of acquiring customers pay off in the first sale. It is *repeat* sales that make new customers valuable.

The value of new customers to an organization easily can be calculated after the initial sale. With a database, marketers can project additional sales—through cross-selling and continuity programs—to predict the lifetime value of these newly acquired customers. At the same time, by collecting information and learning more about current customers' tastes and preferences, marketers can effectively target new customers with the same characteristics. In this way, the organization can not just replace customers lost through attrition but can grow.

Customer "Lists" vs. Customer "Databases"

There are lists, and then there are databases.

A list is commonly thought of as a list of customer names. Sometimes this list includes prospects, or people who have inquired about a product or service.

Often a company with a customer list seeks new customers by renting lists of prospects. Basically, there are two types of rental lists available: lists of people who have responded to other offers (called *response lists*) and lists of people compiled from public sources of information such as automobile and driver's license registrations, membership rosters, or manufacturer's warranties. These lists will be examined in greater detail in chapter 5.

An organization's customer list is its most productive and responsive mailing list. This is because of the very special relationship—or goodwill—that any organization enjoys with its own customers. Of course, active customers—those who have recently bought from the organization—are the most valuable segment of the house list. Of lesser potential, but still more responsive than lists from outside sources, are buyers who have become inactive, those who have inquired but have not purchased, and those who have been referred or recommended by present customers.

House lists are among an organization's most valuable assets, because they generate future business at a much lower cost than acquiring new customers from outside sources. It is not uncommon for a house list to be four, or even ten times as responsive as an outside list with which there is no customer relationship.

The value of any house list can be substantially increased by turning that list into a true *database* of usable customer information. To do so, you need to collect much more than your customer's name and address. A database becomes more useful as it includes more details about the customer's demographics and buying habits. Besides allowing you to sell more goods and services to current customers, a database lets you identify prospects who closely resemble your customers.

Your database can also guide your continuity selling, cross-selling, and prospecting efforts in both an efficient and effective manner. Properly used, a database can help avoid misdirected and cost-inefficient marketing efforts. It can direct and target marketing efforts so that these will be well-received and thus effective.

More than a mailing list, a database is a planning tool. It also provides the means for analysis and evaluation. It enables the direct marketer to dig beyond traditional accounting reports into the intricacies of marketing success.

A Check List of Why You Need a Database

A database can:

- Match products/services to customer wants and needs

- Help you select new lists or use new media that fit the profile of existing customers

- Maximize personalization of all offers or customer contacts to individual customers

- Provide for ongoing interaction with customers and prospects

- Pinpoint ideal timing and frequency for promotions

- Measure response and be accountable for results

- Help you create the offers most likely to elicit response from your customers

- Help you achieve a unique selling proposition (USP), targeted to appeal to *your* customers

- Integrate direct response communication with other forms of advertising

- Demonstrate that CUSTOMERS are valuable assets

What Information Should Your Database Contain?

The core of a customer database is a name and address record which is complete, accurate and well maintained. Beyond that, there is no cut-and-dried checklist stipulating how much information your database should contain or how detailed that information should be. Different organizations have varying needs. Consumer buyers differ from industrial buyers. But this list of essentials can get your database off to a good start. Try to include:

- A unique identifier such as an ID or match code
- Name and title of individual and/or organization
- Mailing address, including ZIP Code
- Telephone number
- Source of order, inquiry, or referral
- Date and purchase details of first transaction
- Recency/frequency/monetary transaction history by date, dollar amounts (cumulative) of purchase, and products (lines) purchased
- Credit history and rating (scoring)
- Relevant demographic data for consumer buyers, such as age, gender, marital status, family data, education, income, occupation, length of residence at address given, geodemographic cluster information, and similar data of value
- Relevant organization data for industrial buyers such as standard industrial classification (SIC), size, revenues, number of employees, length of time in business, perhaps information about the area of the organization's economic/social location, and even information about the personality of individual buyers within the organization.

What data you include depends entirely on its future value in use. "Nice to know" or "we may need that somewhere down the line" are not valid reasons for accumulating data, even though today's technology encourages it. Information costs money and that cost must return a value.

Information is also a perishable commodity. Not only does the degree of customer activity (or inactivity) fluctuate, but the people and organizations comprising your database are far from static. Their demographics change as they get older or raise families. They change jobs, within as well as between organizations. Their attitudes and preferences change. They die. They move. In 12 months, 20 percent of an average customer list could change address.

Such volatility demonstrates the importance of adequate mailing-list maintenance. It demonstrates, too, that customer lists that are mailed to and maintained religiously have greater deliverability value to the direct marketer than do lists compiled without data qualification, from directories or rosters.

Data about customers and their transactions need to be kept up to date. No advertiser, but especially not the scientific direct-response advertiser, wants to distribute communications indiscriminately. It is important to make sure that the message is not only deliverable, but that it is properly targeted. Cost without benefit is to be avoided. To achieve this end, you need to be concerned with mailing list maintenance as well as with ongoing updating of the transaction and other data contained within each customer record.

What Kind of Database Do You Need?

A database can be an added strength to a company's marketing efforts, or it can—as with direct marketing organizations—drive the entire operation. Below are five categories of database development and utilization, with a brief description of each. Decide which of these your organization currently has or needs—then consider how you might develop and utilize your own database further.

The Customer Database

The simplest, yet most important, database may be little more than a collection of customer information. It can be used to identify the company's most valuable customers and communicate with them in ways that—based on their past preferences—are likely to elicit response. Purchase history can be combined with demographic and psychographic data to predict future purchases. This database can further categorize customers as follows:

- *Active Customers:* What actions have customers taken in the past? How recently have they purchased? How frequently have they purchased? How much did they spend? What are their product or service preferences? From what promotion source were they acquired? Identifying your most active customers can help you concentrate your resources on the most profitable segment of your customer list.

- *Inactive Customers:* How long have prior customers been inactive? How long had they been active? What was their buying pattern while active? How were they initially acquired? What offers have they received since? This information can help you design promotions that re-activate your inactive customers.

- *Inquiries:* From what media source did inquirers come? What was the nature and seriousness of the inquiry? Do you have any demographic or psychographic information on inquirers?

- *Referrals:* Who recommended these as prospects? For what purpose? Can the name of the referrer be used in follow-up?

The Prospect Database

The databases of existing customers can enable you to identify new prospects most likely to become customers, and thus begin a prospect database.

- Profile customers in your existing database *first*; then seek prospects like them.

- View such profiles in terms of *lists*—of readers, viewers, listeners—in order to effectively utilize *all* advertising media and not just direct mail.

- Think in terms of *market segmentation and product differentiation.* Then, *position* differentiated products (such as recordings of rock music) to market segments (high school students, for example).

- Employ a *rifle* rather than a *shotgun* approach to prospecting. Aim for *individuals* with similar characteristics to existing customers, not the mass market.

- Experiment with prospect lists . . . *test them.*

The Enhancement Database

Highly sophisticated computer matching technology now permits overlaying one or multiple databases on *your own* in order to transfer relevant information. Database enhancement can substantially increase the amount and quality of information you hold on each customer or prospect.

- In its simplest form, an enhancement might be the addition of age (from a driver's license record) or telephone number (from a directory record). Other possibilities include past transactions; demographic and psychographic data; credit experience, if pertinent; people on the move, evidenced by an address change; significant characteristics of a business; and a multitude of customer behavior and transaction data.

- By overlaying multiple databases, you can eliminate duplications between and among the lists and identify "hotline names" (those who responded most recently) and "multi-buyers" (those who appear on more than one response list).

- Negative screening, such as a credit check, can be used to *remove* a record from a solicitation database.

The Cluster Database

Consider expanding your database using publicly available information on people, groups, and businesses. Certainly a major database for direct marketers is that of the decennial Census of Population and Housing. The Census is particularly useful in explaining the characteristics of a small geographic cluster (such as a ZIP Code area) and from this evaluating a buying environment in order to predict response. Look also at:

- Affinity groups like clubs, associations, neighborhoods where people with like interests tend to cluster. Behavior within such clusters, including buying habits and attitudes, tends to be influenced by these common interests.

- Geographic reference groups small enough to facilitate prediction through environmental demographic databases such as census tracts, block groups, and ZIP Code areas.

- Lifestyle (psychographic) reference groups, having common activities, interests, and opinions.

- Industrial data for business purchasers, including information on such variables as size, sales revenue, number of employees, capital and standard industrial classification (SIC).

The Analytical Database

Use your database not just to collect transaction information and segment your lists, but also to aid decision making—both in marketing and in overall business strategy. Using your database as an analytical tool incorporates the statistical techniques and findings of research as well as the results of testing. It also includes the models you build and the simulations you use to support your decisions.

- Use your database to measure response and keep records for accountability purposes.

- Use it also to analyze, interpret results, and evaluate the effect of every marketing decision you make.

- Then, use it to predict future response.

The Customer Database and the 80/20 Principle

Simply put, the 80/20 principle means that *eight out of ten new things we try fail.* In direct marketing, this means that 80 percent of the new lists, alternative copy platforms, and other "variables" we test are less effective than what we are already doing. That is because what we are now doing represents our cumulative best effort as derived from all of our prior experiences and tests. It takes a lot of "test" efforts in order to beat an established "control" effort that has evolved over time.

The 80/20 principle demonstrates the relationship between marketing effort and result. While the actual percentage will vary among different organizations, it can be shown that 80 percent of a firm's customers do not contribute profit to the same degree as does the other 20 percent. Put another way, 80 percent of the profit in an organization comes from 20 percent of its customers.

Forward-thinking organizations who understand this principle seek out the 20 percent of their customers (or prospective customers) who will contribute the highest returns and direct 80 percent of their marketing effort towards them. Marketing costs can thus be *targeted* in order to maximize profit. Because it can identify both profitable customers and wasted effort, a customer database—properly developed, maintained, and utilized—is the means through which this can be achieved.

Traditionally, marketing costs—and advertising costs in particular—have been viewed as an *expense*. Typically, marketers have used sales history from prior or current sales periods in order to set the marketing budget for the next period. The fallacy of this method of budgeting is that marketing effort comes only as a *result* of sales, i.e., "the more we sell, the more we can spend on marketing."

In direct marketing, where acquiring that 20 percent of customers that brings in 80 percent of the profits is paramount, it makes sense to view the cost of acquisition—i.e., the marketing effort—as a *cause* of sales, and therefore as an *investment*.

WORKSHOP

How to Use a Database to Find Your Most Profitable Customers
THE RECENCY/FREQUENCY/MONETARY (R/F/M) FORMULA

An essential tool for identifying your best customers is the recency/frequency/monetary (R/F/M) formula.

By carrying within each customer's record the date, volume, and nature of purchases, over a period of time, it is possible to determine periodically the performance record of each customer. This enables you to estimate the future potential of that customer, and relate the cost of future promotion to the potential benefit to be derived from each customer in the database. The 80/20 principle in action!

The R/F/M formula is not new. It has been a standard for general merchandise catalogers for half-a-century. Originally developed by George Cullinan for his company, Alden's, this formula has been followed by many others, including Sears Roebuck and Montgomery Ward. To a mail-order customer who complained when he didn't receive a seasonal or sale catalog—or even the "Big Book" mailed periodically—the pat answer was that the customer's R/F/M score didn't warrant the expense of sending it!

The exact R/F/M formulation for each direct marketer will vary according to the relative importance given to each of the three variables:

- the recency of purchase
- the frequency of purchase
- the monetary value of the purchase.

Under certain conditions, there might be a need for further weighting of the calculations of particular promotions that might have more relevance, for example, to customers who had purchased most recently.

Figure 3.1 illustrates the use of the R/F/M formula in evaluating customers in an organization's database according to the combined R/F/M values of their transactions over a period of time. In this hypothetical example, three customers (identified as A, B and C)

FIGURE 3.1

Evaluation of customer database records by recency, frequency and monetary values of transactions (R/F/M).

ASSUMPTIONS:

Recency of Transaction:
20 Points If within past 3 months
10 Points If within past 6 months
5 Points If within past 9 months
3 Points If within past 12 months
1 Point If within past 24 months

Frequency of Transaction: # Purchases within 24 Months x 4 Points each (Maximum = 20 Points)

Monetary Value of Transaction: $ Volume of Purchases within 24 Months x 10% (Maximum = 20 Points)

Weighting Assumption:
Recency = 5
Frequency = 3
Monetary = 2

Customer	Purchases	Recency	Assigned Points	(x5) Weight Points	Frequency	Assigned Points	(x3) Weight Points	Monetary	Assigned Points	(x2) Weight Points	Total Weight Points	Cumulative Points
A	#1	3Mths	20	100	1	4	12	$ 30	3	6	118	118
A	#2	9Mths	5	25	1	4	12	$100	10	20	57	175
A	#3	24Mths	1	5	1	4	12	$ 50	5	10	27	202
B	#1	12Mths	3	15	2	8	24	$500	20	40	79	79
C	#1	3Mths	20	100	1	4	12	$100	10	20	132	132
C	#2	6Mths	10	50	1	4	12	$ 60	6	12	74	206
C	#3	12Mths	3	15	2	8	24	$ 70	7	14	53	259
C	#4	24Mths	1	5	1	4	12	$ 20	2	4	21	280

have a purchase history calculated over a 24-month period. Numerical points are assigned to each transaction, according to a historically derived R/F/M formula exclusive to this organization. Further weighting is given to recency of purchase (times 5), frequency of purchase (times 3), and monetary value of purchase (times 2). Thus, on a scale of 10, recency is weighted at 50 percent, frequency at 30 percent, and monetary at 20 percent.

The resultant cumulative scores—202 for A, 79 for B, and 280 for C—indicate a potential preference for customer C. Based on C's R/F/M history, a greater number of promotion dollars (such as mailing a seasonal catalog) could be justified. Sending a catalog could also be warranted for customer A. Customer B might be an unlikely risk and sending a catalog could be a misdirected marketing effort.

While recency of purchase has been given the greatest weight in this hypothetical example, each organization must determine through its own analysis the factors that influence purchases. As a rule of thumb, however, the buyer who has purchased most recently is the one most likely to buy again.

4

Building a Database

Willie Potts, a salesperson at the Jack Henry clothing store in Kansas City, has—though he does not think of it as such—a customer database. It's a collection of handwritten index cards. Each card carries a customer's name, address, and telephone number written in block letters. Many also have the customer's occupation, spouse's name, and other personal data.

Most importantly, though, Willie lists each suit, each sport coat, each pair of trousers, each overcoat, and each rain coat ever bought by the customer, with details like its color, style, purchase date, and price.

Willie, thanks to his manually maintained database, can not only keep a profile of customers, he can use that profile to anticipate future purchase needs. Having used his database to develop personal relationships with customers, he knows whom to call or mail a simple postcard when an item comes in that he feels will fit the needs of any of his customers. Better yet, he know whom to tell when that expensive Oxxford suit goes on sale!

A database can be as simple as Willie Potts' index cards or, with today's computer technology, its size and sophistication can be boundless. In this chapter, we'll look at the building of a database, beginning with a fundamental question: Where does the information in a database come from?

Sources of Information

Most of the information needed to begin a customer database is readily available within an organization. Accounting records, shipping and fulfillment records, service reports, inquiries, warranty cards, and survey research results can all yield valuable marketing information.

But just because the information is there does not automatically qualify it for entry into a marketing database. Some information is unnecessary; other information is too expensive to acquire. A guideline to follow is this: collect that data you think you'll need to know . . . and no more.

Chapter 3 listed types of information a direct marketing organization might need to know and include in its customer database. For individual consumers, this would generally include, in addition to name/address, information about transactions, and relevant demographics. For business organizations, the names/addresses of decision makers would be augmented with transactions data and relevant information about the organization itself.

Other information may be appropriate for a supplemental database, such as information about undesirable prospects or poor credit risks that you may not want to solicit in the future. Another subsidiary database might categorize and identify ZIP Codes or other geographic areas in which response from prospects is more likely to occur, or even climatic regions most suitable for particular clothing or plant varieties.

In order to identify prospects with the greatest potential to become customers, you may want to rely on an *external* database. Paying to use this kind of database as needed is probably wiser than bringing it in-house where maintenance could be a problem. Compiled lists are a good example of an external source of information that can be rented without acquiring and maintaining data used infrequently.

Information Costs Money . . . But So Do Bad Decisions

The building of a database can represent a considerable investment of both time and money. Information costs money. It is important to consider just what will be done with data once it is collected.

How will the data be stored and accessed? How will it be maintained and kept current? Will it provide benefits at least equal to its cost? Will it aid in decision making? *Will the database be used for analysis and evaluation to lower future costs, as well as creating and cultivating customers to increase revenues?* Information may cost money, but so do bad decisions.

Designing the Database

There are two broad categories of database to consider when you are thinking in terms of reference and retrieval of relevant data: *hierarchical* and *relational*.

Hierarchical Databases

These systems are built around the idea of a *single, central record*. For example, all information relative to an individual customer is contained in a single, master record. There is no need in such a system to cross refer to other data sources. Airline and hotel reservation systems have been developed in this way. While single-record hierarchical databases provide high-volume access and ease of use, their analytical capabilities can be limited by the extent of the data available in such restricted records. An example of a hierarchical data record, with typical information, is shown in Figure 4.1.

Relational Databases

These systems, which are a more recent approach to database development and utilization, provide the advantages of simplicity and flexibility, minimizing redundancy. Related information is drawn from different, independent database sources as needed. For example, a product database can be linked to a customer name/address database in order to direct promotion to those purchasing particular products. At the same time, the separate product file makes possible product-line analysis regardless of customer. Links can be established, too, with billing and/or shipping and inventory records as relevant information is needed.

FIGURE 4.1

Hierarchial format of a single source record.

TITLE

CUSTOMER KEY

ZIP-KEY	LAST-NAME-KEY		

ZIP-CODE	LAST NAME	FILLER	ACCT. CLASS KEY	12X-CODE	INITIALS
X (03) 99	X X (03)	X (04)		9	XX

CUSTOMER NAME

LAST NAME		INITIALS
X (15)		XX

CUSTOMER ADDRESS

ADDRESS 1	ADDRESS 2	CITY	STATE	ZIP	ZIP-FREE
X (22)	X (15)	X (15)	XX	9 (05)	

TITLE

PHONE

AREA	NUMBER
99 9 (05)	9 (07)
FILLER	

MEDIA-TABLE

1	2	3	4	5	6	7	8	9	10

MEDIA-CODE	QTY
X (04)	99

ORDERS

1	2	3	4	5	6	7	8	9	10

PROD-CODE	
X (04)	9 (03)

TITLE

INITIAL-ORDER-DATE	LAST-ORDER-DATE	LAST AMOUNT	TOTAL AMOUNT	NO. OF TIMES ORDERED	PRT CODE
9 (06)	9 (06)	9 (36) 99	9(06) V99	99	9

CHG-ACCT-INED

CHG-NO	EP.	CLUB NO.		
S 9 (17) COMP-3	S (04) SA-5	SP (05) COMP -3		

5	6	7	8	9	10	1	2	3	4

FILLER

Computerizing the Database

Like a boy and his dog, a direct marketer and his or her microcomputer or PC are inseparable. Many successful direct-marketing entrepreneurs have conceived and managed entire mail-order businesses through a personal computer. It has most of the tools needed to run a business: spreadsheets for finance, analysis, and evaluation; word processors for writing letters; desktop publishing for creating catalogs; modems to enhance communications and enable home shopping; and, of course, the tools to develop and utilize marketing databases.

Managing computer technology, though, can be very frightening to the inexperienced. What's more, it is ever changing. But the key players in PC hardware—such as IBM, Apple, Compaq, Dell, DEC, Toshiba and Zenith—are taking huge strides toward making their systems user-friendly and accessible by even the computer novice. By linking more than one system together, PCs are becoming both increasingly powerful and increasingly versatile.

Computer software programs are proliferating at a dizzying pace. There is a software package for almost every operations and applications need of direct marketers: fulfillment, list management, mailing systems, analysis, and evaluation.

Of special interest to direct marketers are the database management systems enabling storage and retrieval of information. Some such systems provide for the retrieval of related records from other databases, i.e., the category of relational databases referenced earlier. There is an abundance of such software programs on the market, including ORACLE, dBase, Paradox, FoxPro, CA-DATACOM/DB, Ingres, and IMPRS. Additionally, word processing software such as Word for Windows and WordPerfect incorporates database and mail/merge features.

Using Merge/Purge and Match Codes to Eliminate Duplication

For best results, a database must be designed so that it eliminates duplicated information and, therefore, wasted marketing effort.

The more that external lists are used to supplement a house list, the more complex this problem becomes. Customer lists from different sources may duplicate each other; response lists and compiled lists may contain a surprising number of duplicates, *within and between* lists; and, many names may already be on your house list. The solution is to use merge/purge and match codes to eliminate duplication on internal lists as well as on external response or compiled lists being used for customer solicitation.

The merge/purge process on computerized databases simplifies the elimination of duplicate records. With merge/purge, it is possible to extract from each name/address record abbreviated information about that record. This abbreviation is called a *match code*, constructed so that each individual record can be compared with every other record in the database. Exact matching of name/address records requires a good deal of computer memory. An *abbreviation*, designed so that the chance two match codes from different records will be the same, minimizes that need. A match code can allow for errors within a record's parts. For example, look at the spellings of the surname in these two records:

Melinda Barton
5410 Salisbury Drive
Lexington, MA 02173

Melinda Burton
5410 Salisbury Drive
Lexington, MA 02173

It is likely that this is the same person. Match codes can be constructed so as to identify this apparent duplication, even though the two name/address records are not identical.

An example of a simple 18-digit match code derived from the name/address preceding is shown in Figure 4.2. Quite often, other data might be added to the match code such as a unique identification (a Social Security number, for example), coded birth date, or expiration date of a publication subscription. Periodical mailing labels often contain match codes of this type.

Through a merge/purge system using match codes, potentially millions of records can be compared at the same time, within and between lists. Duplications are identified for special handling. Figure 4.3, for example, displays multiappearances on two or more mailing lists, with variations of duplicate names/addresses.

The merge/purge process will express the number of duplicates between two lists as a percentage. As Figure 4.4 shows, even a 5 percent "hit" rate can result in substantial cost savings, as 5 percent fewer pieces need to be mailed. The cost savings are substantial when several hundred thousand name/address records are merged and purged. Identification of potential duplication of 15 percent, when one million names on various prospect lists are merged and purged, would result in a reduction of 150,000 pieces of mail. At an assumed cost of $500 per thousand names mailed,

FIGURE 4.2

Mailing list match code.

Position	Item	Description
1	State	A unique alpha-numeric code assigned to each state
2- 5	ZIP Code	Last 4 numbers of 5-digit ZIP Code
6- 8	Surname	1st, 3rd and 4th alpha characters of surname or business name
9-12	Address	House or business street number
13-15	Address	1st, 3rd and 4th alpha characters of street name
16	Surname	Alpha-numeric count of characters in surname
17	Given Name	Alpha initial of first name
18	Given Name	Alpha-numeric count of characters in first name

Example Address	Derived Match Code
Melinda Barton	92173BRT5410SLI6M7
5410 Salisbury Drive	
Lexington, MA 02173	

this results in a mailing cost savings of $75,000. Offsetting this savings, of course, would be the cost of the merge/purge process itself, possibly $10 per thousand names examined or $10,000 for a one million name/address input.

Using Merge/Purge to Find Multibuyers

Besides eliminating duplicate names/addresses, saving money, and sparing customers the irritation of receiving redundant mailings, the merge/purge process offers another, possibly even greater, advantage. If the same name/address is found on two or more cus-

FIGURE 4.3

Merge/purge duplication listing.

Name	Address	City	State	ZIP
Debra Simpson	948 S Ruby Ave	Sober	NJ	08106
Debra Simpson	948 S Ruby Ave	Sober	NJ	08106
Safiyya Sobell	107 Alexander St	Sober	NJ	08106
S Sobell	107 Alexander St	Sober	NJ	08106
R Peters	Apt 902 797 N 6th	Sober	NJ	08106
R Peters	789 N 6th St 63	Sober	NJ	08106
John Ziebart	44 Marsac Pl	Sober	NJ	08106
Walter Ziebart	44 Marsac Pl	Sober	NJ	08106
Horace Roberts	253 N Sixth St	Sober	NJ	08107
Horace Roberts	253 N 6th Apt 2	Sober	NJ	08107
Susie Martin	49 Hawthorne L	Sober	NJ	08107
Susie Martin	49 Hawthorne Lane	Sober	NJ	08107
Susie Martin	49 Hawthorne Ln S	Sober	NJ	08107
Susie Martin	49 Hawthorne Ln S	Sober	NJ	08107

FIGURE 4.4

Economic value of merge/purge of mailing lists utilizing match codes to identify duplication and multibuyers. Assumes mailing cost of $500 per thousand pieces mailed.

	Total Number of Names/Addresses Merged		
% DUPLICATION	100,000	500,000	1,000,000
5%	$ 2,500	$12,500	$ 25,000
10%	$ 5,000	$25,000	$ 50,000
15%	$ 7,500	$37,500	$ 75,000
20%	$10,000	$50,000	$100,000
25%	$12,500	$62,500	$125,000
30%	$15,000	$75,000	$150,000

tomer lists simultaneously, it is conceivable that individual, now identified as a *multibuyer*, is an excellent prospect for future response. Experimentation has shown, in fact, that the expectation of a higher rate of response from those names appearing on three lists is greater than the expectation from those names on two lists. The merge/purge process can identify these special multibuyers for special handling.

Other Uses of Merge/Purge

The merge/purge process can also effectively remove names of individuals who have expressed a desire not to receive particular solicitations, as well as those who have been poor credit risks or are otherwise potentially undesirable customers.

Maintaining Your Database

A database is a perishable commodity. Unless it is kept up to date, information ages. When incorrect addresses or telephone numbers result in misdirected advertising promotions, the cost is twofold: (1) the cost of the wasted contact, and (2) the sacrifice of potential response.

As you design your database, strive to make it easy to maintain. Make sure that information is compiled and developed in a *uniform* manner. Only when such uniformity exists within a computerized list is it possible to use merge/purge or match codes with any assurance of reliability.

Your database will need constant control and maintenance. On a regular basis, you will want to perform the three tasks involved in maintaining a reliable database:

1. Nixie removal

2. Change of address

3. Record status update

Nixie Removal

The term "nixie" refers to mail that has been returned because it is undeliverable as addressed, and no forwarding address has been provided. This might result from a simple error in the street address or ZIP Code. If such an error can be traced, the address can be corrected.

Other possible reasons for undelivered mail are that the person to whom mail is addressed is deceased or has moved and left no forwarding address. In such cases, the person should be removed from the mailing list portion of the database, leaving other records intact until a new address, if any, is known.

Often mail addressed to a deceased person will continue to be delivered to a surviving spouse. Or, mail to an individual who has changed positions or even left an organization will be received by the replacement in that position. Although the Postal Service will not send notifications in such instances, experienced direct marketers obtain list corrections through specially directed mailings. Or, if a salesperson from the firm calls on the customer, corrected information can be obtained that way.

Other ways in which mailing lists can be updated to avoid "nixies" include references to news items as well as references to public records such as birth and death notices, marriage and divorce (annulment) proceedings.

Change of Address Update

Whenever possible, address corrections should be requested through the Postal Service. Mail prepaid with first-class postage is automatically returned if undeliverable or forwarded without charge if the new address is known. For a fee, the sender will be notified of the new address as well.

The U.S. Postal Service offers a variety of address correction procedures for third-class advertising mail. Most notable is the computerized National Change of Address (NCOA) file which virtually all major mailers, and a goodly number of minor ones, use regularly.

Direct marketers themselves often encourage those on their databases to inform them of any change of address or telephone number, and provide the means for doing so.

Record Status Update

It is of vital importance to keep the record status of customers always up to date.

New transactions from customers should be entered into the database promptly, as they have major impact on the R/F/M formulation described in chapter 3. They also influence the success of future solicitations.

Above all, direct marketers do not want to distribute their direct response advertising indiscriminately. They want to make sure not only that their messages are delivered but that they are delivered to the right prospects at the right time.

Database Security

Like buildings, equipment, and inventories, computer databases are assets. Unlike more tangible assets, they are somewhat more portable. Millions of records can be packed on a single reel of computer tape or even on a pocket-sized cassette. Their loss or misuse through falling into the wrong hands can be highly detrimental to the organization. But unfortunately, because their value is intangible, they are not easily insurable, except for replacement and duplication costs.

For these reasons, special precautions must be taken to prevent destruction, loss, theft, or unauthorized use. Attention should be given to:

- Program administration, assigning responsibility for development, modification, and utilization

- Limiting exposures through secured location, proper storage, controlled access, cryptographic techniques, adequate erasure, and destruction

- Marking the list, to discourage unauthorized use

- Discouraging theft through visible security, awareness of misuse precautions, apprehension of violators

- Maintaining accountability for systems and documents.

The logical first step is to make sure the database is stored in a manner that protects it against natural hazards of fire and water damage, as well as theft or unauthorized use. To discourage theft, access to list files should be limited and controlled at all times. Should a list be lost, either inadvertently or through improper handling, duplicate records should be available at a remote location.

A variety of marking techniques have been developed for "seeding" mailing lists. In the event a list is misappropriated or misused, such decoys—which are either incorrect spellings or fictitious names that are known and appear nowhere else—can identify misuse. These don't, however, always lead to the culprit!

Certain mechanical or cryptographic precautions can be taken to discourage theft, such as passwords or a connecting procedure from the end of one tape reel to the beginning of the next.

Any storage or list marking efforts should be communicated to all involved in database handling so that each person will be aware of these.

Privacy and Confidentiality

They know about you.

They know how old you are. They know if you have children. They know about your job.

They know how much money you make, what kind of car you drive, what sort of house you live in and whether you are likely to prefer pâté de foie gras and champagne or hot dogs and a cold beer.

They know all this and much, much more. And do you know how?

They know your name.

What they have done with it is very simple. They have added it to a mailing list.

— *The Kansas City Star*

Most people (even direct marketers themselves!) will admit that unsolicited, irrelevant, direct mail can be a nuisance. Some regard it as a trespass on personal privacy. And there have been cases in which unscrupulous retrieval of data, which itself might possibly be inaccurate, has resulted in damaged reputation or even physical harm.

Contrary to commonly held beliefs, though, direct marketers do not disclose such confidential customer information as income level, how much money each has in savings, how deeply in debt each is, or what their personal habits and attitudes might be. In fact, such information is very rarely available to direct marketers . . . or anyone else for that matter.

On the other hand, information such as actions taken, memberships, age, sex, etc., is very likely available. Yet, to reveal the age of an addressee on an envelope enclosing a relevant insurance offer, visible to the mail carrier and others, could very well be considered a breach of confidential information.

Similarly, an insurer who knows of a policyholder's hearing impairment should not make this confidential fact known to, say, a hearing aid dealer. On the other hand, less sensitive information might easily be shared. The subscribers to a travel magazine might well appreciate being solicited with an offer of luggage for their next trip.

The 1977 618-page *Report from the Presidential Privacy Protection Study Commission* concluded that the appearance of an individual's name on a mailing list was not in and of itself an invasion of privacy, so long as that individual had the prerogative to remove it from that list.

In reaching this conclusion, the commission observed "that the balance that must be struck between the interests of individuals and the interests of mailers is an especially delicate one." The commission also noted the economic importance of direct mail and its social use to "create diversity in American society." And, it agreed that the *receipt* of direct mail was not really the issue, but rather how the mailing list record of an individual was being used.

Following the urging of the Commission to minimize the intrusiveness and nuisance created by unwanted and irrelevant direct response advertising, the Direct Marketing Association established self-regulatory guides and programs. These include the Mail Preference Service and Telephone Preference Service, which enable name removal from member mailing lists when so requested. Most catalog merchants, publishers, and other direct marketers now also provide the means for their customers to opt-off solicitation lists.

Intrusion vs. Relevance

Henry David Thoreau, who once contended that nothing worthwhile ever arrived in the mail, continues to live on, thanks to the Thoreau Lyceum in Concord, Massachusetts. His quest for privacy and a totally natural lifestyle alongside Walden Pond, however, little prepared him for the computer-generated letter from a local automobile dealer which was addressed to "Mr. Lyceum Thoreau."

Similarly, the apartment dweller who received an offer of "A Limited Opportunity To Be One of the First American Gardeners To Grow and Enjoy the World's Largest STRAWBERRIES" wondered "where they got my name" and considered it junk mail. So did the executive invited to attend a conference, half way around the world in Singapore, of an industry with which he had no connection. The TV cable householder invited to add a premium channel for which he or she was already paying wondered why. And, the individual with no pets who received a catalog of pet products thought, "This catalog is irrelevant, its receipt is an intrusion and an invasion of my privacy!"

The marketing purpose of a database is to acquire and serve customers efficiently and effectively through selectivity. It is *not* to increase the volume of advertising intrusion but rather to confine promotion to that which is relevant. By carefully segmenting markets and relating past preferences and buying behavior to future needs, the database works to minimize such intrusion.

WORKSHOP

How the Stash Tea Company Built a Customer Database

This chapter began with a description of some key sources of information for building of a customer database. After you've read what Stash Tea Company did, see what other ideas you can come up with as an extension of its successful actions.

Stash began in 1972 in the basement of a Victorian house in Portland, Oregon. Its tea products were sold in small volume to restaurants and institutions, with accelerated growth coming from distribution through supermarkets.

Here, however, it was almost impossible to break through shelves crowded with better-known brands, especially when Stash Tea cost about 20 percent more than its competitors. Stash reported that although it enjoyed a 75 percent share of specialty teas served in restaurants in Oregon, it attained only a 17 percent share in supermarkets working through distributors.

Contrary to traditional distribution practiced by packaged goods companies, moreover, Stash shied away from "awareness" advertising and did no cents-off coupon promotion. Rather, it created awareness of its brand through advertising on the small tag of the tea bags provided to diners in restaurants. These diners, it is said, rarely specified brand as much as they did blend!

These small direct-response print ads were coupons offering to send the respondent a catalog of many varieties of teas and related tea products. (Similarly, labels stuck on Vidalia onions in stores asked buyers to "Call 1-800-VIDALIA for a catalog.")

From 3,000 leads monthly, the conversion to buyers of those sent Stash Tea catalogs reached 25 percent, one-third of these ordering from the initial catalog. In a short time, mail-order buyers exceeded 150,000. The database thus built was then shown to food distributors and retailers to convince them to stock Stash Tea.

Do you feel that mail-order distribution, to force grocery store distribution and enhance restaurant sales, via a database, was a waste of time? "Pete" Hoke, publisher of *Direct Marketing*, who first reported this case, pointed out that Stash—

- built a list to which new products could be tested
- derived customers for personal sales follow-up
- created a catalog to display the entire line, which stores could or would not
- created a catalog to "teach" about its products
- implemented a "member-get-a-member" affinity group through its catalog
- was able to merchandise store locations through its catalog
- was able to feed mail-order results to retail stores
- detected viable new product directions
- was able to interact multiple channels

That's quite a list of accomplishments for one modest effort.

5

Enhancing a Database and Finding New Customers

A customer list becomes a database when it is *enhanced* to include more than simply a name, an address, and a telephone number.

It is enhanced when it records relevant information about each customer's *transactions*.

It is further enhanced when *demographic and/or psychographic* information is appended for each consumer or industrial buyer.

Enhancement of a database can also include *environmental* information such as data about ZIP codes for consumers or about Standard Industrial Classification (SIC) codes for businesses.

In essence, enhancing your database lets you learn *more* about your customers and why they buy—so you can nurture your relationship with them for many profitable years.

How to Profit from an Enhanced Database

Any organization must first know about its own customers. This knowledge not only opens up the opportunities for continuity selling and cross-selling. It also is the prelude to pinpointing prospects most likely to become customers in the future.

A simple five-step sequence can help an organization profit from enriching its database:

1. Identify your customers

2. Enhance your database

3. Overlay environmental data

4. Utilize the tools of prediction

5. Utilize your own analytical database

These five steps can mean the difference between a profit and a loss in any enterprise. Building and enhancing a database is a *means*. It is not an *end* in and of itself. The true end is the success and stability of the enterprise.

Step One: Identify Your Customers

Many well-intended marketers spend considerable time and money on seeking new customers, without first learning about the characteristics of their present customers.

By answering some basic questions about your customers, you can more easily (and less expensively!) find others like them. Who are your customers? Where are more like them to be found? How were these customers obtained? Which offer the most opportunity from continuity sales and cross sales? How much can be spent to acquire them; what is their lifetime value?

These are the questions that your customer database, when enhanced, can answer.

Step Two: Enhance Your Database

First of all, make sure that you have a proper mechanism for the development and maintenance of your database. Then, capture customer information that is relevant for pinpointing future revenues. This includes product(s) purchased, recency/frequency/monetary and other transactions data. It also might include significant demographic data derived from databases external to the organization.

Step Three: Overlay Environmental Data

Certain kinds of environmental data can help you predict future purchasing behavior. Perhaps the characteristics and variables within ZIP code areas influence response. (The case at the end of this chapter discusses some of those variables.) Or industry characteristics of a business firm may impact response. Environmental data can be geographic, demographic or psychographic, in that it can be a predictor of lifestyle and buying behavior.

Step Four: Utilize the Tools of Prediction

Develop high regard for and a comfort level with numbers and statistics. Not every technique is complicated. At the low end, a simple response percentage can highlight the most productive segment of a response list. At the high end, a complex, multi-variate regression analysis can correlate response variances with the behavioral variables found within a cluster of ZIP code areas. These tools will be discussed at length in Part Three, *Customers: Where They Are*.

Step Five: Utilize Your Own Analytical Databases

Most response-oriented direct marketers experiment a lot. From these tests, they collect a great deal of data. Properly analyzed, such data can provide much guidance. Databases should contain more than "nice to know" information. They should tell you who your best customers are, where they are and how to cultivate them. Such analytical databases, too, should track the lifetime value of a customer, because what better way is there to set promotion budgets for new customer acquisition?

A Guide to an Endless Array of Enhancements

Your database may already contain proprietary information such as actions taken, product preferences and credit worthiness. But you may want to add information such as age (from a public record compilation of driver's licenses), a mobility indicator such as length of residence (from a telephone directory compilation), or a credit rating (from a credit rating bureau).

Your database can also be used as a *negative* screen, to suppress promotion to those desiring not to be solicited (from the Direct Marketing Association's mail and telephone preference compilations) or an address where a prospect no longer resides (from the United States Postal Service's NCOA file).

All of this information is available from compiled lists, response lists, and credit reporting databases. But before you turn to external data sources, take a second look at your own files. Believe it or not, an insurance company once surveyed its policyholders to determine their ages, forgetting that it already had this information in its underwriting database!

Compiled Lists

Carefully developed and maintained name/address compilations can be a key source of data. This information can be transferred to customer or other response lists to segment and qualify them.

There are a great many compilations available, ranging from those owned by large list compilers like Metromail and Donnelley Marketing, whose lists contain information on millions of U.S. residents, to smaller lists of individuals or organizations shown in trade, professional, or membership rosters.

While such information—directory listings and license registrations, for example—are matters of public record, often clearly visible, there is a great deal of concern by privacy advocates over the potential harm from its transfer. Potential misuse of data, even breach of confidentiality, should, per the marketer who keeps customers' best interests in mind, override the need for targeting relevant products and messages to likely prospects.

It behooves those who access such information, therefore, to be responsible in its acquisition and use. It helps to think about data as a means to define market segments, rather than as a way to single out an individual. For example, knowledge of age of a cluster of individuals can be a legitimate means to direct advertising for certain offers, thus minimizing waste as well as avoiding intrusion of those to whom the message is not relevant. On the other hand, specific reference to an individual's age, even on a direct mail envelope where it is visible to others, can result in resentment toward the marketer and be seen as a breach of privacy.

Telephone Directory Compilations. Drawn from white pages (individuals) or yellow pages (organizations), these enormous databases can yield a treasure trove of information.

For households, you can estimate household mobility, identify multi-unit buildings or associate the address itself with a ZIP Code or other small geographic area for which census data is obtainable. Phone numbers can be added where worthwhile.

For businesses and other organizations, you can discover Standard Industrial Classification codes by cross-referencing Yellow Pages categories. You can determine the year the organization first appeared, or identify a franchise such as McDonald's, a brand affiliation such as General Electric, or membership in a professional society. As with households, telephone or FAX numbers can be appended. The extent of Yellow Pages advertising can be identified, too, if relevant to response.

Telephone directory compilations can themselves be enhanced from other databases and usually are. Gender can be approximated from first-name tables; ethnicity can be approximated from surname tables. Telephone surveys of directory listings of organizations provide names/titles of decision makers, number of employees, sales volume. First-time listings—of households on the move or of business start-ups—can be isolated as well.

City (and/or Criss-Cross) Directories. Where available, these household compilations can augment telephone directories, which omit both those who lack telephone service and those who, through their own choice, prefer not to be listed. City directories are typically compiled through mail survey or house-to-house canvass. They often list all persons in the household, along with age, marital status and family relationships. Children are included as are senior citizens living with their children.

City directories are readily obtainable for manual perusal, and they are often incorporated into the enormous databases offered by major list compilers.

Voter Registration Files. Like city directories, these are locally compiled, typically by county election boards or commissions. Like city directories, they include many individuals who may not appear in telephone directories. But, they are far from comprehensive. Not all U.S. residents are citizens and, of those who are, not all are registered as voters.

Voter lists may show party affiliation, an important qualifier for political parties and candidates, although party affiliation may not always be current. Addresses may also be out of date if the voter has not voted recently. For these reasons, voter lists are probably most effectively used when they are joined with other databases by a professional compiler.

Real Estate Records. Information derived from public real estate records can provide considerable enhancement to a customer database, especially when offers relate to home furnishings, maintenance, gardening and/or landscaping.

Available data, for either customer enhancement or prospect qualification, includes: type of dwelling unit (single or multi-family, condominium), month and/or year purchased, market value, and residence of owner.

Rosters. The membership rosters of the local PTA, service clubs, neighborhood and trade associations, professional societies, and special interest groups may be a useful source of customer and prospect information. The key qualification is the nature of the group with which an individual or organization is affiliated.

Because rosters are typically in hard copy, working with them can be cumbersome. Duplication may result when an automated means for merge/purge is unavailable. Roster information may not always be up-to-date, and many groups frown on their use as mailing lists.

Still, the information in rosters, especially evidence of affinity with a particular group and its interests, can be a worthwhile enhancement to a customer database. Sizable collections of rosters, drawing together local groups, are available in computer format.

Automobile and Driver's License Registrations. Obtained from the various state motor vehicle departments, registration records can provide year, make and model for each automobile in a household. They can also identify new vehicle purchasers, and, because certain vehicles can be associated with certain lifestyles, offer clues about a customer's lifestyle. The number of vehicles owned in a household, as well as their combined market value, can also be discriminate variables

Since automobile registrations are recompiled annually, they can be used to update mailing addresses. Not so driver's license registrations, which are issued for as many as five years.

However, driver's license registrations are a good source of age and gender information as well as height and weight statistics that can be important predictors of interest in products such as large or tall clothing sizes. A driver's license record can also indicate some degree of physical mobility and acuteness, important qualifiers for products such as insurance.

Lifestyle Compilations. Generally derived from warranty registrations returned to product manufacturers or from survey responses, this information comes from consumers themselves and often provides a variety of demographic data about individuals and households. Psychographic data volunteered by respondents also provide indicators of activities, interests and opinions. Coupled with environmental data obtainable for ZIP Code areas, such databases become valid measurements of lifestyles.

Tens of millions of records, compiled month-to-month and regularly maintained through address correction procedures, comprise these lifestyle databases. Dozens of activities and interests from antique collecting to wildlife/environmental issues can be identified. Included are such diverse indicators as bible/devotional reading, casino gambling, snow skiing, gardening, motorcycling, and watching TV sports.

Demographic selections from such databases often include gender, title, age band, home ownership, marital status, income, occupation, credit card usage, children at home, education, religion, and ethnicity.

Direct marketers who effectively use lifestyle compilations as mailing lists will often initially transfer relevant variable information from these databases to their own customer records. Thus, they can model their customer penetration correlated with these variables so as to predict the likelihood of response to their offer from segments of the multi-million compilation. These segments become key sources of new customer acquisition.

Credit Reporting Databases

Major national credit-reporting organizations offer a broad array of enhancements and qualification screens, negative as well as positive. Their databases let you suppress promotion efforts to those with poor credit records, and properly direct promotion efforts to those qualified for and likely interested in a particular offer. They are also excellent sources of up-to-date, deliverable addresses, because they are updated every month as consumers and businesses pay their bills.

A great deal of the demographic data offered as mailing lists by credit-reporting organizations is derived from sources external to them. For consumer records, this includes a variety of information about those in the household as well as the housing itself. For business records, primary and secondary industry classifications are shown, as are other non-confidential data derived from survey or observation.

The use of information from credit-reporting databases is, in the eyes of consumers and consumer advocates, controversial—especially when it is used for offers that do not grant a credit privilege. That is why highly personal and confidential information obtained in the process of credit checking and reporting is available to credit grantors only.

On the other hand, credit organizations have *modeled* the likelihood of bankruptcy without individually identifying those bankrupt. Without breaching individual confidentiality, this kind of modeling with predictive averages is a valid enhancement for a customer database as well as an important qualifier for an offer to be directed to a prospect mailing list.

Respondents to Direct Offers

Experienced direct marketers know that the single most important qualification of a mailing list is history of response.

Response or action taken can be *predictive*. It can help a direct marketer predict whether a prospect might make similar or related purchases in the future. A purchaser of a travel cruise to Alaska, for example, might be a more likely prospect for a world cruise than one who had bought a weekend Caribbean cruise. By enhancing your database with information from other response lists, you can learn a great deal about customers without invading their privacy.

Conducting a merge/purge of several response lists against each other and your own customer list can offer further predictive likelihood by identifying multi buyers. Large database compilers have facilitated this by marking mail-order buyers from many,

many individual response lists and identifying them by purchase dollar range and purchase method. In doing so, they have coupled the typically larger numbers of records available in compiled lists with qualifications of mail responsiveness, recency of purchase (hotline buyers) and frequency of purchase (multi-buyers). The result is the best of both worlds: high volume and great qualification.

Compiling a Customer Profile

The primary reason for enhancing your database is to develop an accurate profile of your customers—a profile you can use to identify prospects that are like the most profitable of the customers you already have.

Organizations have in the past developed cursory profiles of their customers through primary research, surveying a sampling of them in order to determine their key characteristics. Today's database and analysis technology, however, provides opportunities for statistical modeling which can embrace not just a sample but the entire customer file. Further, it can categorize these customers by product(s) purchased, by recency/frequency/monetary analysis, by credit experience, and by a host of transactions variables. Then, it can relate its findings to an infinite array of enhancements: geographic, demographic, and psychographic.

Because today's organizations—their product and promotion strategies, their databases, their markets—are dynamic, customer profiling through statistical modeling needs to be a never-ending process. As was emphasized in Chapter 4, *Building a Database*, the collection and analysis of information costs money and should be undertaken only if benefits derived from better decision making exceeds these costs.

A starting point for developing customer profiles is through the calculation of *market penetration*. This, in its simplest form, is a percentage relationship of customers to some benchmark universe. It tells what percentage of the total universe of potential buyers are *your* customers. To be even more predictive, such arithmetic should be performed on customer segments: R/F/M categories, product lines, specific demographics.

The benchmark universe can be as broad as a total population or a count of all households or of all families. It may be as narrow as a count of mailings of a particular promotional effort to a particular list. Industrial organizations might view their prospect universe as all firms within a Standard Industrial Classification (SIC), within a size category or within a geographic area. The universe could be even further refined by age band, marital status, occupation, educational level, or by numerous other restrictions.

When determining percentage penetration of customers in a potential market it is well to keep in mind the "equal effort over time dilemma." You may have a higher concentration of customers in a particular segment—high-income households, for example—simply because your prior marketing efforts, for a good many years, have been directed to that segment. Without objective guidance, you may have unintentionally bypassed even more productive, lesser-income segments.

A solution to this dilemma is to measure a controlled universe such as a direct-mail effort across all household income segments with response key-coded by income category.

Suppose that you mail an offer to 19,600 households, each identified as falling into one of four low-to-high income ranges: A, B, C and D. You receive 350 responses to your offer, an average of 1.79 percent response. When the response is tabulated by household income range, market penetration is shown to increase as household income increases:

Household Income Segment	Total Mailed	Total Responses	% Response to Mailed
A	5,793	60	1.04
B	2,735	33	1.21
C	6,731	138	2.05
D	4,341	119	2.74

From this table, it is readily apparent that the response rate from the direct-mail offer is positively correlated with household income. That is, the response rate increases along with household income. Since the market potential has been defined with a direct-mail effort sent to all available households irrespective of income, our market penetration, viewed as a series of response rates, is controlled. Thus, we are not faced with the "equal effort over time dilemma."

Now, let's assume that we have a list of 350 customers, who were acquired over a period of time from a market potential universe consisting of 19,600 households. Let's change only the column headings on the preceding table so it looks like this:

ZIP Code Cluster	Total Households	Total Customers	% Customers/ Households
A	5,793	60	1.04
B	2,735	33	1.21
C	6,731	138	2.05
D	4,341	119	2.74

What we are showing here is a clustering of 350 customers according to their ZIP code locations and calculating the percentage of customers we have among all households in those ZIP code clusters. Once again we see that market penetration increases from A to B to C to D. What we *don't* know in this instance, however, is *why!*

If we had the means to correlate our customer penetration of the market potential of the four ZIP Code clusters, we ought to be able to seek prospects and more readily convert these to customers in cluster D than in cluster A. The trick is to know what distinguishes D from A . . . demographically, psychographically, and geographically.

Try eyeballing the ZIP code clusters in which you have the greatest market penetration. What is *different* about each ZIP code area? Are they rural or metropolitan? Are the housing structures multifamily? Are the neighborhoods "new" or "old?" Are the household heads young or old, college postgraduates or high school dropouts? You might even look at a census of population and housing. From all of this data, it may be possible to discover what distinguishes the high penetration areas from those with low penetration.

Using Customer Profiles to Find New Customers

A customer profile—real or estimated—is the starting point in seeking out new prospects or prospect lists!

Response Lists

Response lists of other organizations, whether rented or exchanged, can be a valuable source of new customers like those you already have in your own database.

The source of the response list is the first indicator of how productive it will be for you. The more similar the owner-organization's product, service, or market to your own, the better. The prospects in the list are more likely to match your customer profile and are therefore more likely to respond to your offer and thus become your customer, too.

Recency of purchase by prospects within the response list is a powerful qualifier. Concentrate your first test efforts on any prospect list on the so-called "hotline" names, those who have responded to the list owner in the most recent 30, 60, or 90 days. Recent *repeat* buyers should respond even better. If that segment doesn't attain needed response, it is unlikely going any deeper into the list would be worthwhile.

Segment the list also by product or service purchased. A customer purchasing fishing equipment from a mail-order catalog could be a likely prospect for a fishing magazine. A small business subscribing to a periodical for those who work at home could be a potential buyer of office supplies, computing equipment, or furniture.

You can also select names using age, gender, and other demographic data, or geographic selections that match your customer profile. Select from response lists those areas in which you have the greatest penetration in your own customer list.

Compiled Lists

Compiled lists that have been carefully segmented have been known to generate response rates that exceed response-qualified lists. They present an advantage to mailers seeking responses beyond the bounds of available response lists.

Consider generating an indexed market penetration analysis of your customers against the compiled list. A customers/ households indexing might look like the one below. Length-of-residence of a household is estimated by the number of years a telephone directory listing has appeared at the current address:

Length-of-Residence	Number of Households	%	Number of Customers	%	Customer %/ Household %
1Year	10,000	32.26	100	10.00	31.00%
2 Years	9,000	29.03	150	15.00	51.67%
3 Years	7,000	22.58	200	20.00	88.57%
4 Years	4,000	12.90	250	25.00	193.80%
5 Years	1,000	3.23	300	30.00	928.79%
Totals	31,000	100.00	1,000	100.00	

From this analysis, it is apparent that customer penetration is positively correlated with length-of-residence at an address. Similar market penetration analyses might be drawn from other compiled lists, i.e.:

- Make, model and year of automobile registered

- Age as given on a driver's license

- Assessed valuation, as shown on a property tax record

- Political affiliation, as shown on a voter registration

- Standard Industrial Classification

- Yellow Pages advertising, listing classification(s) as well as the extent of display advertising.

Frequently, too, warranty card disclosures that include lifestyle indicators such as hobbies, interests, activities, and ownership can be used for segmentation purposes.

CASE STUDY

How Old American Insurance Company Benefited from an Enhanced Database

Old American Insurance Company of Kansas City, Missouri, had been for more than 25 years a mail-order direct marketer of insurance, primarily to senior citizens, when Medicare was introduced in 1966. The Medicare program, an adjunct to Social Security, was designed by the federal government to provide for the health care needs of those persons age 65-plus as well as those younger persons suffering from a disability entitling them to receive Social Security benefits.

The introduction of the Medicare program held both negative and positive implications for the future course of Old American's business. But, because its mail-order products had historically been viewed as *supplements* to basic coverages, the firm was as interested in researching what Medicare did not provide for as well as what it did.

Research soon revealed that Medicare fell far short of perfection. Its shortfalls—broadly divided between the expenses of hospital confinement and other medical expenses including that of care by physicians—were categorized as these: (1) deductibles; (2) coinsurance; (3) non-covered services; and, (4) billing beyond charges defined as reasonable. Because Old American Insurance Company had established early in its history an objective of providing *supplemental* personal insurance coverages to older Americans, it now developed a product line to *complement* the Medicare program.

Old American Insurance Company had already developed an extensive database of older-age active policyholders, lapsed policyholders, beneficiaries, referrals and inquirers. It had compiled a proprietary database of prospective policyholders and had conducted extensive testing of response mailing lists it had pinpointed within the well-defined senior citizen market segment.

Promotion of the Medicare supplement new product line began simultaneously with the advent of the federal program. Because of significant database availability, the primary advertising medium was obviously direct mail. Testing revealed that selected magazines and newspapers directed to older persons were successful, as was selective TV and radio.

During extensive experimentation, it was learned that market segmentation needed to go beyond simply an age variable. Old American developed its Lifestyle Market Segmentation model to increase the effectiveness of its reach. This model took advantage of the new postal ZIP Code by enhancing all of its senior citizen databases, customers and prospects alike, with environmental data just becoming available for ZIP Code areas.

Use of the Lifestyle model demonstrated conclusively that not all persons 65-plus behaved the same way as buyers. The rural and urban buyer, for example, had different preferences. Those who after retirement had moved to high-rise apartment buildings in central cities behaved differently from those who had moved to sunbelt communities. Both prospect groups, in turn, responded differently from those seniors who had chosen to remain in their old neighborhoods.

Following extensive research, Old American developed a statistical profile of those persons over age 65 who would be most likely to respond to its offers and then validated this model through test mailings. Prospecting was then confined to only those ZIP code areas with a high response propensity. Benefit-oriented direct-mail copy was directed to these selected market segments. Cost savings resulting from elimination of non-productive mailings justified the cost of database development and profiling while higher response rates increased profits.

This case study of Old American Insurance Company, serves as a real-world demonstration of both the power of database and the opportunities database enhancement provides.

PART

III

Customers: Where They Are

How do you find, from among prospects, more customers like the most profitable of those you already have? *How do you replace productive customers lost through attrition? How does your organization find new customers in order to grow?*

In Part III, we will cover the steps involved in identifying and finding those customers: segmenting markets, and conducting and evaluating the surveys and tests that contribute to our knowledge of our customers and markets.

All of these areas require a healthy respect for both research and statistics—areas that make chills run up and down the spines of many direct marketers.

Customers are not numbers. But numbers can optimize the creation and cultivation of customers. That is why the process of creating and cultivating customers is aided and abetted by an understanding of research and statistics. If we get to know our customers with a statistically significant degree of assurance, we can then provide them with meaningful benefits—and they'll keep coming back.

6

How to Segment Markets

Meet Bob Martin, an "average" consumer. He has a job, a home, a car, a spouse, and about 2 1/2 children.

Somewhere in the depths of his consciousness, he is dimly aware that he probably needs what you have to sell.

You'd like to have Bob Martin as your customer.

To reach Bob Martin, you need to know about him. You need to know his geographic, demographic, and psychographic qualifiers.

It could be helpful, too, to know about actions he has taken in the past, even his transactions with other organizations.

And does he have an association, *an affinity,* with a group?

This chapter shows how to use the principles of market segmentation to *find* Bob Martin and others matching his profile. For business-to-business direct marketers, this chapter is concerned with finding data-defined industrial organizations.

What You Should Know about Consumer Market Segmentation

A *market* is defined as customers with needs and/or wants to satisfy, money to spend and the willingness to spend it.

A *target market* is a group of customers or prospects to whom an organization specifically aims its marketing effort.

A *market segment* is a homogenous subgroup of a heterogeneous aggregate market which is selected as a target market.

A *cluster* is a grouping of smaller entities, such as ZIP Code areas or comparable individuals, into a market segment.

Like direct marketing itself, market segmentation is a customer-oriented philosophy. In market segmentation, one thinks in terms of a "rifle" taking aim, contrasted to a "shotgun" scatter to an aggregated, or mass, market.

With a rifle, one *targets* a prospect. With a shotgun, one *includes* a prospect, who is then called upon to identify himself.

One can position and create advertising for a mass medium like television so that it appeals to a market segment. But, oftentimes much of this advertising will fall on deaf ears, as it reaches all in seeking only those who are qualified prospects.

Your database is the "rifle" that lets you avoid this scattershot approach. By enabling you to pinpoint prospects that match the profile of desirable customers, your database lets you create promotions for *specific* market segments. Far from falling on deaf ears, your message has a greater chance of being listened to and heeded.

The broad consumer market contains an infinite number of subgroups. These clusters of buyers or prospective buyers can share geographic, demographic, or psychographic characteristics that can be identified using segmentation techniques. Figure 6.1 provides an array of many such characteristics.

Geographic Segmentation

Geographic segmentation techniques seek to identify whether a prospect or customer resides in an urban or rural area, and pinpoint the region, state, county or metropolitan area where he or she lives.

United States geographic groupings range from the country in its entirety down through nine census regions, and 12 Federal Reserve districts. Beyond these are 50 states, 3,042 counties and 435 congressional districts.

Then, there are endless arrays of state-defined areas of economic-activity and trading areas. Overlapping these are an abundance of so-called media communication areas and retail trading zones associated with cities, towns, rural farm and rural non-farm areas. Smaller geographic units include census tracts containing clusters of block groups and individual city blocks.

FIGURE 6.1

An array of characteristics describing consumers within market segments.

DEMOGRAPHICS

Personal Information:
Age:
Gender:
Height:
Weight:
Eye Color:
Hair Color:
Race:
Ethnicity —
— Foreign Born:
— Country of Origin:
— Mother Tongue Spoken:
Religion:
Marital Status:
Family Size:
Education Level:
Occupation:
Industry:
Income:
Mobility:

Dwelling Information:
Type (single/multiple):
Size (square feet):
$ Value (if owner):
$ Rent (if not owner):
Structure Age:
Tenure of Residence:
Household Equipment —
— Dishwasher:
— Clothes Washer/Dryer:
— Refrigerator/Oven:
— Computer:
— VCR/Camcorder:
— Freezer:
— Television:
— Radio:
Structure Equipment —
— Heating:
— Cooling:
— Multi-Bath:
— Public Water:
— Public Sewer:
— Security System:
Kitchen:
Direct Access:
Telephone:
Autos Registered:

GEOGRAPHICS

Location Information:
Nationality —
— United States:
— Other American:
— European:
— Asian:
— Australian/New Zealander:
— Other:
Metropolitan Type —
— Urban:
— Suburban:
— Urban Fringe:
— Rural Farm:
— Rural Non-Farm:
Region:
Federal Reserve District:
Congressional District:
State:
County:
State Economic Trading Area:
Media Communication Area:
Retail Trading Area:
Metropolitan Statistical Area:
Census Tract:
Minor Civil Division:
Block Group:
Block:
Block Face:
ZIP Code Area:
Telephone Area Code:
Latitude/Longitude Coordinate:

PSYCHOGRAPHICS

Attitudes:
Interests:
Opinions:
Activities:
Biological Needs:
Psychological Motivations:
Environmental Influences:

ACTIONS TAKEN

What Purchases Lately:
What Lists On:
What Affinity Groups:
What Favorite Charities:
What Political Affiliation:
What Influencers:

There are numerical codes, too, such as ZIP codes, telephone area codes and route numbers. Mind-boggling as it is, the Census Bureau's TIGER (Topologically Integrated Geographic Encoding and Referencing) system has assigned latitude/longitude coordinates to one hundred million street addresses for site locations!

Geographic information can tell a lot about a market segment, because people with like interests tend to cluster. Their buying decisions are often influenced by a desire to emulate friends, neighbors, and community innovators. The ZIP code and other geographic indicators provide the means to identify clusters of households that have a high degree of homogeneity so that marketers can make use of a consumer's urge to "keep up with the Joneses."

Demographic Segmentation

Demographic statistics include age, gender, marital status, occupation, and education. They are generally compiled for a geographic area, and are frequently related to some social or economic characteristic or to a comparison over time. The primary unit of observation in demography is the individual, with the family unit (related individuals living together) and/or the household (families plus individuals living alone plus non-related individuals living together) being secondary.

There are three main sources for demographic data:

- By enumeration of a population as in a census

- By registration on the occurrence of an event such as birth, marriage, or death; by recording a purchase such as real estate or an automobile or by application for licensing

- By sample surveys or tabulations of special groups.

Often, *change* in demography is important. If a single person marries or if a baby is born, these events have significance for certain marketers. So do population change, or high mobility of the residents of a geographic area. Direct marketers capture such major events so as to offer differentiated products to geographic or demographic market segments.

Psychographic Segmentation

Much recent market segmentation is based on psychographic factors associated with a certain lifestyle. Knowing a prospect's personality, behaviors, and "AIO"—attitudes, interests and opinions—can help you understand customers who share geographic and demographic characteristics, but have different buying behaviors.

Psychographic and lifestyle information can be obtained from the interaction of demographic variables and geographic locations. It can also be determined from actions taken, such as subscribing to a certain publication, or owning a certain product. Survey responses can also demonstrate attitudes, interests, and opinions.

One means of psychographic market segmentation is The Lifestyle Selector®, compiled by National Demographics and Lifestyles, Inc., Denver, Colorado. This database is developed from consumer-product registration questionnaires packaged in a wide variety of hard goods provided by more than 75 companies, with permission for mailing list use granted by the respondent.

The Lifestyle Selector comprises 25 million households, about 25 percent of all U.S. households. More than a million questionnaires are received monthly, so the database is self-perpetuating. Each household record contains selected geographic and demographic data together with more than 60 lifestyle selections and dimensions, all as reported by the respondent.

It is thus possible for a consumer direct marketer to develop a profile of an organization's own customer list through computer matching with The Lifestyle Selector. This profile, then, can extend the organization's prospect base through use of similar names within the total 25 million household database.

Another way to discover psychographic characteristics is to watch for multiple-list identifications. For example, a registered owner of a particular automobile, residing in a 90-unit apartment building located in an affluent ZIP code, might also appear as a subscriber to *The Wall Street Journal,* a customer of L. L. Bean. and a contributor to the Republican Party and Planned Parenthood. These multiple-list identifications can describe attitudes, interests and opinions—and provide names and addresses of prospects to boot!

Segmentation Based on Actions Taken

Market segmentation based on actions taken is the way direct marketers have traditionally selected from an endless array of response mailing lists. Among such lists in consumer markets are buyers of all types of products, subscribers to specialized magazines, members of differentiated book and record clubs, donors to causes, collectors, and members of organizations.

Lists of respondents are enhanced when there is an affinity, a relationship, a membership, a loyalty to the organization.

They are enhanced, too, when subgrouped by characteristics of recency, frequency, and monetary. Recent "hotline" buyers of books about the Civil War are a segment within a segment. So are those who have been buying the annual update of an encyclopedia for ten or more years. So are those who buy "the best."

Likewise, those who send gifts to others, as opposed to buying for their own consumption, are a segment within a segment. So, too, are those who purchase as members of a select "club."

So is the very large segment of "Conscientious Wheelers and Dealers"—the millions of people who enter contests and sweepstakes, solve puzzles, buy lottery tickets, and order "genuine synthetic diamonds!"

At heart, every mailing list represents a market segment—a segment that has demonstrated its interest in certain offers by acting on them.

CASE STUDY

Consumer Market Segmentation

Stoney Creek is a residential community located 35 minutes from Charlottesville, Virginia. It is part of Wintergreen, a highly regarded family resort that encompasses 11,000 acres of land centered in the Blue Ridge Mountains, adjacent to the George Washington National Forest, quite near Shenandoah National Park.

While the mountain resort today attracts vacation skiers and golfers from as far away as Washington, D.C. and Charlotte, North Carolina, a major part of its use is by the owners of condominiums and single family residences there. These property owners in effect own the resort, through an organization called Wintergreen Partners, Inc.

The market for Wintergreen residence units has been well-defined and segmented geographically, demographically, and psychographically. The more than 2,000 mountain condominiums at present sold as quickly as they were planned and built. Most of the 500 homes on the mountain have been custom-built by owners.

In the 2,000-acre valley development known as Stoney Creek, nearly 200 single-family units, virtually all custom-built and nearly all primary residences, are occupied year-around. The geographic, demographic, and psychographic mix of these Wintergreen Partners is, however, quite diverse! While some view it as a retirement community, most do not. Many have full-time occupations.

Stoney Creek has succeeded up to now in attracting both retired and working individuals, many of the permanent residents having upgraded from part-time condominium status. Could there, however, be a potential market segmentation conflict here?

One market study conducted years earlier for a condominium retirement community revealed some public misconceptions and prejudices toward these. Respondents to this survey viewed a particular community as an "old people's home," clearly identified with the retirement, perhaps even the nursing home, market. Most respondents, regardless of their ages, just did not think they were "old enough" to move there yet.

In the study, many associated the community's activities and facilities with regimentation and even institutionalism. Some saw it as "not quite respectable" and suggested that the residents were probably shiftless and hedonistic. They used words like "playground," "leisure-living," "fun," and "pleasure," respondents apparently drawing these words entirely from the community's own advertising. The majority of the respondents identified the community as an expensive, high income, high cost place to live. They used these words in an unfavorable sense: "exclusive," "luxurious," and "country-club atmosphere."

That development company learned that buying a home and moving were emotion-laden activities and that different segments of the total market had substantially different motives for changing residences. Unfortunately, it also appeared that the motives of various segments were often at cross-purposes, so advertising appeals to one segment may well alienate other segments.

While Wintergreen has been eminently successful, the Stoney Creek residential community now evolving may have to identify and select those market segments that are most compatible.

How to Identify Industrial Market Segments

In the United States, there are at least ten times as many purchasing households as there are industrial organizations, and about twenty-five times as many individual consumers. But when the customer characteristics of consumer and industrial markets are compared, as shown in Figure 6.2, striking similarities emerge. Information about an individual purchaser is similar whether the person is acting on his or her own behalf, or that of an organization. Information about organizations, though, needs to be obtained through a different set of segmenting tools.

Standard Industrial Classification (SIC) Coding System

A common means of industrial market segmentation is through the Standard Industrial Classification (SIC) coding system developed and maintained by the federal government.

The SIC coding system is used to designate industry groups by function and product and, in a way, parallels the demographic characteristics of consumer markets in that these codes are commonly used for market segmentation and analyzing demand.

FIGURE 6.2

Similarities between consumer and industrial markets.

CONSUMER	INDUSTRIAL
Name/Address	Name/Address
Source code	Source code
Age	Year started
Gender	Gender of decision maker
Income	Revenue
Wealth	Net worth
Family size	Number of employees
Children	Parent firm or subsidiary
Occupation	Line of business (SIC)
Credit evaluation	Credit evaluation
Education	Education of decision maker
Urban/rural resident	Headquarters/branch
Own or rent home	Private or public ownership
Ethnic group	Minority ownership
Sex	Sex of decision makers
Interests	Interests of decision makers
Lifestyle of ZIP area	Socio-economics of location
Mail respondent	Mail respondent
Transactions & R/F/M	Transactions & R/F/M

The first two digits of the four-digit code indicate a major classification of industry, of which there are ten:

01–09	Agriculture, Forestry and Fisheries
10–14	Mining
15–17	Construction
20–39	Manufacturing
40–49	Transportation, Communications, Public Utilities
50–51	Wholesale Trade
52–59	Retail Trade
60–67	Finance, Insurance, Real Estate
70–89	Services (including medical, legal, schools, churches, social services and non-profits)
91–97	Public Administration
99	Non-classifiable Establishments

The final two digits of the four-digit SIC code classify individual organizations by subgroup and further detail within industry. For example, SIC #2300 identifies manufacturers of wearing apparel. Within this classification, SIC #2311 identifies men's suit and coat manufacturers, as detailed here:

SIC #	DESCRIPTION
2300	Apparel and other finished product mfrs.
2310/2320	Men's, youths' and boys' clothing
2311	Suits and coats
2321	Shirts except work shirts
2322	Underwear and night wear
2323	Neckwear
2325	Separate trousers and slacks
2326	Work clothing
2329	Clothing not elsewhere classified
2330	Women's, misses' and juniors' outerwear
2331	Blouses and shirts
2335	Dresses
2337	Suits, skirts and coats
2339	Outerwear
2340	Women's, misses' and juniors' undergarments
2341	Underwear and night wear
2342	Brassieres, girdles and allied garments
2350	Hats, caps and millinery
2353	Hats, caps and millinery
2360	Girls', childrens' and infants' outerwear
2361	Dresses, blouses and shirts
2369	Outerwear, not elsewhere classified

Input-Output Matrices

Input-output matrices, derived basically from Census Bureau data, trace the distribution of goods from their origin to their destination. In such a matrix, an industry (SIC) appears as both seller and buyer in row and column headings. At the point where the row and column of any two industries intersect, the matrix records the transaction between those two SIC classifications.

Input-output analysis, in its broader form, thus determines the impact that specific industries have on the total economy, in what they sell and what they buy. A decrease in sales of new automobiles, for example, would result in reduced purchases from the tire industry. This, in turn, would result in reduced sales by the tire industry and would ultimately reduce the tire industry's purchases from the rubber industry.

The Census Bureau's TIGER System

The Census Bureau's TIGER (Topologically Integrated Geographic Encoding and Referencing) system, an address coding guide associating latitude and longitude coordinates with street addresses, can be used to pinpoint geographic locations, establish business sites, locate competition, measure distance, and generate data about the demographic environment of a business location.

Coupled with mapping capabilities and drawing on information from its customer database, a business-to-business direct marketer can effectively visualize reach and penetration of its geographic territories, as a sales management tool, with TIGER.

Business Clusters

As with consumer markets, industrial markets can be clustered and defined by ZIP code area. Data by SIC classifications have been associated with ZIP code area data. Ruf Corporation, Olathe, Kansas, has also identified ZIP code areas in terms of economic activity (number of businesses, commerce input-output, bank savings, retail sales, etc.) as well as in terms of consumer demographics and lifestyles (number of households, home value, income, autos owned, etc.) Ruf's business clusters reveal the impact these variables have on the buying behavior of businesses located in these areas.

Other Industrial Market Segmentation Criteria

Industrial organizations can be categorized by financial strength or size as well as in terms of number of employees and/or sales volume. Geographic selectivity is often used, too, including city size and location.

Other criteria differentiate whether the enterprise is a headquarters or branch office, a parent or a subsidiary. There can be selection by form of ownership, also. A proven predictor for many business-to-business direct marketers, too, is the extent of telephone directory Yellow Pages advertising.

Direct marketers must appeal not only to organizations but also to relevant individuals within these organizations. Demand within industrial organizations is not generated by purchasing agents alone. More likely, joint decisions are made by engineers, chemists, architects, production managers, and a host of other specialists. Personalities and demographics of these decision makers and influencers is now becoming a basis for market segmentation, also.

Some public-sector organizations can be described in the sense of industrial markets. These include medical and health services, legal services, schools, libraries, social services, churches, and cultural and arts organizations.

But the most important basis for business-to-business market segmentation is still an industrial organization's own database. Its own customer list, including prior brand and product purchase behavior, actions taken, credit evaluation, recency/frequency/ monetary scoring, and each customer's own enhanced demographic profile, offers the most accurate means of targeting relevant industrial market segments.

CASE STUDY

Industrial Market Segmentation

FedEx is an air courier delivery service with its headquarters in Memphis, Tennessee. It uses its own fleet of airplanes and trucks to transport letters and packages. At night FedEx planes leave key cities throughout the country, carrying letters and packages from those origination airports. These converge on Memphis, where cargo is sorted, reloaded, and flown out for delivery early the next day at destination locations.

FedEx markets and prices its delivery in a number of categories, depending on type, weight and delivery service. A few years ago, one of its most profitable categories was called Priority 1. This category included the delivery of nearly any shape or size package weighing between 5 and 70 pounds. Because Priority 1 had become a popular and profitable product, FedEx's competitors offered similar services.

To expand its market, increase its penetration, and hold its present customers, FedEx decided to increase its own promotion of Priority 1 and announce a new discount pricing schedule for it. Transaction data was used to define three market segments for the direct-mail promotion program:

1. Frequent users of Priority 1: 29,126 customers

2. Infrequent users of Priority 1: 121,705 customers

3. Non-users of Priority 1: 63,431 customers.

The symbol used to dramatize the 5- to 70-pound Priority 1 service was a 5-pound exercise weight. Frequent users of Priority 1 received the exercise weight immediately as a goodwill gift; infrequent users had to request it; nonusers received it as a premium with a purchase of Priority 1 service for the first time.

Frequent users were asked to identify other prospects and decision makers in their organizations. A total of 7,044 (24.18%) of the 29,126 frequent user recipients of the promotion did so.

Of the 121,705 infrequent users contacted, a total of 25,985 (21.35%) responded requesting the gift. In the process, they supplied 14,723 names of new prospects in their organizations.

Of the 63,431 non-users of Priority 1, a total of 9,300 (14.66%) purchased the service and submitted a copy of the FedEx air bill as proof to receive the exercise weight.

Market segmentation of the FedEx customer database according to prior transaction information proved to be a viable and profitable means of cultivating present customers in order to promote a new product. A total of 21,767 new prospects were identified and there were 9,300 proven sales, totalling $500,000 in revenue, to *new* users of Priority 1 service.

7

What You Need to Know about Research and Testing

Direct marketers, in their quest to know their customers, collect vast amounts of information. They need to know how information is gathered, synthesized and analyzed in order to extract exactly the right data to segment markets, construct offers and create new customers.

In order to use information, direct marketers need to be comfortable with certain research, testing and statistical systems and methods. This doesn't mean knowing exactly how to calculate the limit of error of an experiment, or how to compute a chi-square test. But it does mean knowing the basic principles involved in constructing and interpreting surveys and tests.

When you know how to use these tools, you can direct your promotional efforts to prospects who are likely to respond to your offers. This minimizes unwelcome intrusion on unlikely prospects— and increases effectiveness and efficiency by lowering the costs of the overall promotion.

When to Use Research and Testing

Research and testing can be used whenever a direct marketer faces multiple options and needs to decide which one to pursue. It can help direct marketing managers seek solutions to problems, or become knowledgeable about the options facing them. It can help relate risks to rewards and estimate the profit impact of making the *wrong* decision.

Research can take one of three primary forms:

1. *Exploratory research* is designed to develop a hypothesis of some sort. This "pilot project" approach can take the form of test mailings, surveys, and in-depth or focus-group interviews.

2. *Descriptive research* uses a "logical reasoning" approach to draw conclusions from observed facts such as census data, surveys and polls. If a population increase is observed, for example, the researcher may reason that the market is now larger.

3. *Causation research* relies heavily on historical data and statistical techniques to follow a cause-and-effect approach. For example, a regression analysis can relate the demographic composition of a ZIP code area (the cause) to the response rate from a direct mailing to that area (the effect). Difficult and costly, this form of research embraces much of the database analysis used in direct marketing.

Because research itself is an expense, it must provide benefits that justify the expected costs. Potential risk must be related to potential reward. Three criteria can determine whether research information is valuable to a business decision:

1. The degree of uncertainty regarding the outcome of various courses of action

2. The economic consequences of making a wrong decision

3. The amount by which the information, if obtained, is expected to reduce the initial uncertainty.

Direct marketers use the term "uncertainty" in a statistical sense to describe a lack of advance knowledge of the outcome of an action. Uncertainty is thus a risk. Research and testing attempt to reduce (but not eliminate) uncertainty to a manageable risk in order to eliminate undesirable alternatives, such as unprofitable mailing lists, from all those being considered.

Research can help answer questions about many aspects of direct marketing. In deciding the extent of advertising effort, research can help establish how the advertising budget is to be determined, whether it should be a *result* (based on actual past sales) or a *cause* (based on objective future sales), and whether expected results warrant estimated costs, and anticipated rewards outweigh potential risks.

Research can help decide how a budget will be allocated, which products will be offered and at what prices, which market segments will be selected, and what blend of offer, copy, graphics, and media will generate the best results.

Direct marketers turn to research for *quantitative* as well as *qualitative* answers. Quantitative research analyzes population sizes, numbers of transactions, and other data to tell you who, where and how many prospects you have. Qualitative research tells you about buyer behavior. It offers reasons why people and organizations buy.

Testing involves experimentation. In direct marketing, testing most often means offering a product or service for sale and then measuring those who actually respond. Survey research might identify those who *say* they would respond if given the opportunity. Experimentation through testing, on the other hand, measures those who actually *do* respond.

In short, research and testing can help direct marketers make decisions based on facts, not hunches. While it is not a substitute for sound executive judgment, it is a great decision-making aid. Knowing how to use the tools of research and testing can help you make valid decisions, spending time and money wisely.

Data: Types, Sources, and Collection

Information is all around us, if we would but recognize it, collect it, catalog it, and refer to it. The trick is to determine *what* information is needed, *where* and *how* to obtain it, and then *what* to do with it.

Information—data—is the key to research. After a problem is structured or an objective is defined, data is needed in order to derive the action plan.

Data is usually categorized into two broad groups. *Primary data* is collected for a specific research need, either through personal, telephone, or mail surveys, through observation or through experiments conducted in either a field or a laboratory environment. Primary data is expensive and should only be collected when no *secondary data* is available. Secondary data is that which was collected originally for another purpose but has relevance to, and is available for, the research needs of others.

Secondary data is available from many sources, including your own database. Figure 7.1 lists a variety of sources of secondary data. Before you invest in collecting primary data, make sure you are not "reinventing the wheel." It is conceivable that someone, possibly even your own organization, has already traveled the road you propose to travel.

FIGURE 7.1

Some sources of secondary data.

A. The Organization's Own Internal Records

B. Government Sources: Federal, State, Local

    1. U. S. Department of Commerce
      — Bureau of the Census

    2. U. S. Department of Labor
      — Bureau of Labor Statistics

    3. U. S. Department of Agriculture

    4. Other U. S. Government Sources
      — President's Office
      — Congress
      — Treasury Department
      — Interior Department
      — Health & Human Services Department

    5. State and Local Governments
      — Economic Surveys
      — License Registrations
      — Tax Records

C. Trade, Technical, Professional and Business Associations

D. Private Research Organizations

E. Foundations, Universities and Other Nonprofits

F. Libraries, Public and Private

G. Advertising Media

H. Financial Institutions and Utilities

Primary data is collected through the survey methods shown in Figure 7.2. Interviewing respondents can yield valuable information, including:

- *Actions:* What respondents have done or are doing

- *Intentions:* What respondents expect to do in the future

- *Motivations:* What reasons respondents give for acting

- *Attitudes, Interests, Opinions:* Respondents' views

- *Psychological Traits:* Respondents' state of mind

- *Knowledge:* How respondents perceive specific offerings

- *Socioeconomic Factors:* Age, income, education, etc.

Survey research attempts to observe and record various activities as they naturally arise in the environment. What respondents *say* and what they *do,* however, are sometimes contradictory. In one survey, a large majority of respondents answered "no" to the question, "Would you purchase life insurance by mail, without the guidance of a personal agent?" Yet, every one of these respondents *had* purchased life insurance by mail from the company conducting the survey!

By contrast, experimentation focuses on *results,* not *opinions.* In an experiment, one or more controllable factors (called independent variables) are manipulated to determine their influence on various events or outcomes (called dependent variables) such as the response to an advertised offer. The results are measured in an environment that the experimenter creates and in which controls serve to pinpoint the cause of behavior differences among respondents.

A survey that asks prospects if they *intend to buy* can be translated into direct marketing offers in which the prospect is *asked to buy.* This kind of testing is the form of experimentation favored by direct marketers.

FIGURE 7.2

Primary data collection methods.

Format	Advantages	Disadvantages	Applications
Personal Interview	Provides a complete and accurate sample and complete information. Allows questions to be structured to fit the situation; high response is virtually assured.	Expensive, and the interviewer may create bias that can influence the subject. Interviewers require supervision and control to standardize handling, and avoid cheating. Not statistically quantifiable; projections are subjective.	Used to ascertain attitudes and motivations, on a one-to-one controlled basis, for background information and for generation of ideas about future actions.
Telephone Interview	Fast, economical, can easily reach a representative sample; non-response is low; easy to get respondent's participation; can coincide with other activities, such as TV viewing.	Excludes unlisted numbers except in random-digit dialing. Information may be limited and certain types of questions cannot be used.	Used to increase number of one-to-one interviews when in-depth research is not necessary.
Focus Group Interview (Unstructured small group of subjects converse in a relaxed environment)	Great sounding board for product benefits and promotion features. Good for idea generation and creative evaluation.	Cannot be scientifically controlled and findings cannot be measured or projected. Interaction can sometimes influence participants.	Used chiefly as a sounding board, to obtain reactions; to generate ideas.
Mail Questionnaire	Provides great versatility at relatively low cost. No interviewer bias; no field staff required. Respondents may remain anonymous	High rate of non-response; often requires follow-up. Results may show bias. Surveys can take a long time to develop and even the	Used to maximize number of observations and to provide more valid basis for projection.

FIGURE 7.2 (CONTINUED)

Format	Advantages	Disadvantages	Applications
Mail Questionnaire (Continued)	and replies can be confidential; response can be timed to the respondent's convenience.	best questions may be misunderstood when interviewer is not present.	
Observation (In-store, in-home audits, recording devices, and direct observation at point of sale)	Removes respondent bias.	Opportunities to use this technique are limited.	Used to obtain objective findings, even though opportunities for use are limited.
Dry Testing (Sending out promotions for a product being contemplated, but not yet available)	May help measure potential interest in a product yet to be introduced.	Product may be misrepresented, need to promptly return remittances. More costly than a survey.	Used as a test, with the inherent advantages of an experiment.

The Decision-Making Process

Four steps are involved in using research and testing to make a decision or to solve a problem.

Step 1: Determine objectives. Is the objective increased sales volume, increased response to advertising, greater return on investment, accelerated cash flow?

Step 2: Array alternatives. What are the possible courses of action? How can these best be evaluated, including (but not limited to) such statistical techniques as decision trees, payoff matrices and mathematical models?

Step 3: Deal with uncertainty. How can one assign probabilities, based on judgments, simulations, and statistics, in order to arrive at a proper choice?

Step 4: Perform evaluation. How does one determine the alternative, from all those available, that best suits the objective under conditions of uncertainty? Then, how do you implement it, monitor it and provide for feedback?

The case of the Entrepreneurial Raincoat Vendor illustrates this decision-making process. A middleman who purchases raincoats from an overseas manufacturer for $10 each then resells them to his customers at $35 each through a general clothing catalog mailed seasonally. For a particular seasonal catalog promotion, he needs to decide how many raincoats should be purchased in order to maximize profit. Since the raincoats are distinctively styled, it is assumed that, if they are not sold, they have no further value. The condition of uncertainty in the equation is the weather: will it be a rainy season?

Following the steps of the decision-making process, the entrepreneurial raincoat vendor arrays the following:

- *Objective:* Maximize profits through proper determination of how many raincoats to buy for resale in a seasonal mail-order catalog

- *Alternatives:* (1) Buy 100 raincoats at $10 each; sell them at $35 each; gross profit is $2500. (2) Buy 200 at $10 each; sell them all at $35 each; gross profit is $5000. (3) Buy none, leave the item out of the catalog and avoid the uncertainty (risk) entirely.

- *Uncertainty:* It might *not* be a rainy season. If the mail-order merchant sells only 50, gross profit would be just $750 on the purchase of 100. There would be a *loss of* $250 on the purchase of 200! (Example assumes no later salvage value.) The *probability* that it will *not* be a rainy season is calculated to be 40 percent.

- *Evaluation:* The three alternatives assumed, along with the associated probabilities of rain, are arrayed in the form of the Decision Tree and Pay-Off Matrix in Figure 7.3. This example is simplified to facilitate understanding. In reality, there could be an infinite number of purchase alternatives and a great many other uncertainties, such as timely delivery of the catalog, economic conditions and competition. Of course, promotion cost of the catalog also needs to be considered.

FIGURE 7.3

A simplified example of decision making: The Entrepreneurial Raincoat Vendor.

Decision Tree:

Pay-Off Matrix:

Alternative	Probability	Profit	Expected Value	Risk	Attitude
Buy 100:	40%—No Rain	$ 750	$ 300	$ 0	Play it safe; earn a
	60%—Rain	$2500	$1500		modest profit
			$1800		
Buy 200:	40%—No Rain	($250)	($100)	$250	Take a risk; earn a
	60%—Rain	$5000	$3000		higher profit
			$2900		
Buy 0:	40%—No Rain	$ 0	$ 0	$ 0	Do nothing; lose/
	60%—Rain	$ 0	$ 0		gain nothing

In the Pay-Off Matrix shown in Figure 7.3, the amounts contained in the column headed "Expected Value" are derived by multiplying the percentages shown in the "Probability" column by the corresponding amounts shown in the "Profit" column. From this calculation is derived the *expected* profit under each condition of uncertainty for each alternative given. In one instance, the column headed "Risk" displays a $250 loss in the event that 200 raincoats are purchased and there is no rain.

The "Attitude" column displays how an individual's own intuition might influence what action would be taken. Such models as these do not recommend an action—but they do provide the basis on which to make a decision that fits comfortably with one's own tolerance for risk.

Using Models

The results of research and testing through experimentation can be represented with models like that of the Entrepreneurial Raincoat Vendor. Such models can be used to explain, predict or solve problems.

Models that *explain* can provide descriptions, frameworks and aids to systematic thinking, discussion or hypothesis testing. Models that *predict* can help explain the impact that injection of simulated variables might have on end results. And models that *solve problems* can help facilitate the decision process involved in, say, determining how many telephone communicators and 800-service telephone lines are required to handle high-traffic periods of response to seasonal mail-order catalogs.

Modeling techniques in use today can accurately correlate market penetration with census demographics, lifestyle research, transactions data, and buyer behavior. These models can very accurately predict response from selected market segments of prospects. Statistical decision-support models can build probability profiles of those most likely to respond to an offer. All models, whether used for explanation, prediction or problem solving, rely heavily on the concept of *causation*.

In Figure 7.4, a model illustrates the differences in response between certain demographic segments of a list. The response rate from those persons on the list identified as "older age" is somewhat higher than that from those identified as "younger age." The response rate seems to increase even more among "older age" persons who are also "widowed." It thus appears that "older age" and/or "widowed" marital status are the *cause* of higher response. The higher response could also be the *effect* of mailing only to older-aged persons who are also widowed.

The model, representing response percentages from 28 cells of a total mailing, is called a 4 x 7 matrix. The four columns each represent a marital status, the seven rows each represent an age band. A

FIGURE 7.4

Response rates illustrative of differences in age and marital status within a broad-based compiled mailing list.

Age/Marital Status	Single	Married	Widowed	Divorced
Under Age 30	.53%	.64%	.87%	.56%
Ages 30-39	.75%	1.40%	1.50%	.85%
Ages 40-49	1.03%	1.75%	1.95%	1.09%
Ages 50-59	1.10%	1.80%	2.05%	1.15%
Ages 60-69	1.30%	1.92%	2.23%	1.32%
Ages 70-79	1.36%	2.03%	2.38%	1.40%
Over Age 79	1.42%	2.56%	2.72%	1.50%

response percentage is given where each column intersects with each row. This intersect point is called a cell.

This model is relatively simple to construct. To build it, each segment of a prospect list was key-coded on the response device, so that all responses could be apportioned to 28 cells representing all possible combinations of age and marital status.

How to Design an Experiment
Using Control and Randomization

In an experiment, the *independent* variable is the factor manipulated: a change in the nature of the product or service and/or the way it is offered, a price change, or a change in the promotional strategy employed.

Generally, only one independent variable should be measured at a time. Advanced statistical techniques such as multivariate correlation and regression analysis, though, offer opportunities to measure the interaction of many independent variables simultaneously. (These will be discussed at length in chapter 8.)

Typically, in the direct marketing environment, the *dependent* variable is a statistical measurement of the *result* of manipulation of independent variables. Depending on the structure of the test, that could be expressed as—

- The rate of response to an offer

- The cumulative penetration of a market segment

- Favorable or unfavorable reactions to a product

- The overall rating of a brand preference.

Theoretically, you can test anything. But it isn't a good idea to spend time and money testing insignificant factors. Direct marketers should test only *important* variables—products, offers, media, formats, or timing. Mail-order marketers of an earlier time tested many relatively insignificant factors such as the color of ink used for a letter's signature, or the type of covering used on a window envelope. Resist the urge to be "test happy." Confine your tests and experiments to the big factors that affect your bottom line.

In order to have confidence in the results of a test, you need to design an experiment that adheres to established standards of *control, randomization* and *sampling.*

Valid experiments are characterized by:

1. The presence of a control group, along with the one or more test groups, on which an experiment is not conducted but which is otherwise identical to the test groups.

2. Random assignment of subjects to groups so that differences in composition between the control and test groups occur by chance alone.

3. A sample that is of an adequate size and so drawn from a population that the results of the test, when known, will be statistically valid at a confidence level and an error limit acceptable to the researcher.

The mathematician Blaise Pascal employed the principles of control in 1648 when he hypothesized that atmospheric pressure declined with increasing altitude. Pascal took two barometric readings: the first in his village; the second, an hour later, from the top of a 3,000-foot peak. The second observation did indeed show significantly lower atmospheric pressure. What Pascal did not know, however, was whether the atmospheric pressure had become lower at the bottom as well as the top of the mountain during the hour that it took him to climb there.

Pascal wisely changed his experimental design. He calibrated two barometers before he began his trek up the mountain. At the precise time he read the barometer at the top of the mountain, another villager read the control barometer at the bottom. His comparison, now with a control, showed that although both barometers had lower readings at the end of the hour it took him to climb the mountain, the barometer he carried to the top had a significantly lower reading.

An experiment without control is frequently invalid. A beer distributor hypothesized that an increasing level of advertising expenditure (the independent variable) would result in increasing sales (the dependent variable). Over a 13-week period, the distributor increased the amount of advertising each week. Sure enough, sales increased each week. Overlooked, however, was the simultaneous increase in heat and humidity during the three summer months of the experiment. The distributor's control should have been a measurement of the sales trend, without an increase in advertising, during the same 13-week span in a comparable market with similar climate.

In direct marketing, the effect of an experiment is the difference between the observation of the dependent variable—for example, response rate—after the experiment and the observation of the response rate of the control group, which did not receive the experimental treatment of, for example, a different offer. But the control group is hard to beat, because it represents the cumulative best that an organization knows how to do at any point in time. That is why, as the search for something better continues, eight out of ten trials will not beat the control.

In a well-designed experiment, one has complete control over what is tested and the manner in which the experiment is conducted. But neither the marketplace nor human behavior can be controlled. Seasonality may affect sales, human behavior may be inconsistent. And the actual level of response to an experiment, even when meticulously controlled, may not always be projectable into an unknown future environment. For example, the environment in which the experiment is conducted may not precisely compare with the environment of the continuation effort. Economic conditions or consumer optimism may change. Competition may heat up due to new models and competitor innovations. These uncontrollable factors may affect the test so that, while the *relationship* between a test and its control may be the same, the entire level of response *for both* may be higher or lower than originally experienced.

Designing a Random Sample

Sampling is a method of choosing observations from which an estimation can be predicted. Without adequate sampling, the resultant prediction will be invalid. Direct marketers must know the major means of selecting samples of potential respondents from a population, a database, or a list.

At minimum, the direct marketer should be able to draw adequate samples from a population, and to compute sample sizes, variances and confidence levels. It is also helpful to be familiar with the key terms shown in Figure 7.5.

To assure that experimental and control groups are as nearly alike in makeup as possible, any differences between the two groups should be attributable to chance alone. These are the major ways to obtain such samples:

- *Simple Random Sample:* Using preprinted tables or computer-generated random numbers assures the equality of probability of sample selection. Each consecutive selection, ideally, is made randomly from a population from which the immediately preceding selection is removed. Statisticians call this "drawing without replacement."

- *Systematic Random Sample:* Starting with a random number, every nth name is selected in the proportion that the desired sample represents of the total population. This is technically not a pure random sample, but, it is the sampling method most likely used by direct marketers.

- *Stratified Random Sample:* The names in this selection are drawn in proportion to a particular parameter of a population; i.e., a distribution of the sample by age is proportioned to the known distribution of the population.

- *Cluster Sample:* Area clusters are picked at random and the entire cluster is selected; i.e., the entire ZIP code is an nth selection of all ZIP codes. This technique is convenient when responses are to be followed up in person, to minimize travel time.

- *Replicated Sample:* Several independent random samples are drawn, such as first choosing a stratum from among all 50 of the United States; then choosing a stratum of census tracts within counties of those states. A variation would be selections over periods of time.

FIGURE 7.5

Definition of terms.

Accuracy   The difference between the sample statistic and the actual population parameter.

Bias   A methodical error that occurs in selection of respondents or measurement, i.e., the difference between the expected value of a statistic and the population parameter estimated by the statistic.

Mean   The arithmetic average; measure of central tendency.

Median   An average, the mid-point of values; also a measure of central tendency.

Mode   An average, the value that occurs most frequently; also a measure of central tendency.

Parameter   A characteristic of a population.

Population or *Universe* or *Sampling Frame*   The total domain or group of items being considered.

Random Event   An occurrence which has several possible values and occurs with some definable frequency if many repetitions are undertaken.

Reliability   Standard error of a statistic; its precision.

Sample   Subsets of the total population, for which data are available.

Sampling Error   The difference between sample result and the population parameter (which most often is unknown). Sampling error declines as the sample size increases, assuming an unbiased sampling procedure.

Sampling Method   The means of obtaining a sample from a population.

Simple Random Sample   Every possible sample of equal size has an even probability of selection.

Standard Deviation   A measure of dispersion; square root of the variance.

Statistic   The characteristic of a sample.

Valid   A statistic without bias.

Variance   A measure of dispersion about the mean.

- *Sequential Sample:* Using this method, projection is evolved from progressive data; i.e., selection is based on prior predictions. This is the manner in which political election outcomes are projected by television news teams.

It is possible that the arrangement of a list from which a sample is to be drawn could itself bias the selection. Sequencing of a list alphabetically by surname, for example, could result in ethnic concentrations within certain initial letters. A similar problem could occur when a list is arranged geographically (such as urban/rural) so that location differences are concentrated. Lists arranged in ZIP code sequence allow nth name selection without undue bias.

Sampling error can occur when not everyone in the population of interest is available for selection. Names drawn from a telephone directory compilation which includes neither households without telephones nor unlisted numbers are not representative of a total population. Sampling error might also occur if a sample includes nonprospects; for example, obtaining a sample from a list that includes apartment dwellers to test a lawn furniture offer. Nonresponse error occurs when an individual is included in the sample but, for one reason or another, is not reached or else refuses to respond.

How to Determine the Size of the Sample

Sample size is influenced by two major considerations:

1. The cost involved in reaching the sample

2. The need for enough responses to be able to predict future response within a comfortable limit of uncertainty.

The size of a sample can be determined by a "judgment call" but the scientific basis for sample-size determination is found in probability theory. The "law of large numbers" assures us that, as sample size increases, the distribution of sample means (response rates) concentrates closer to the true mean (response rate) of the total population from which the sample is drawn.

Further, the "central limit theorem" assures us that, in a number of random samples taken from a population, the sample means (response rates) tend to be "normally" distributed.

Commonly called a "bell-shaped curve," the shape of such a nor-

FIGURE 7.6

A normal distribution.

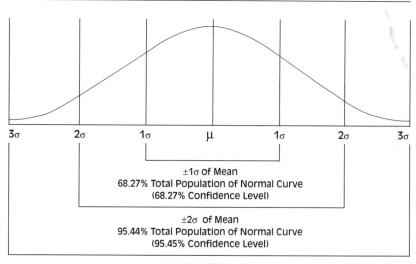

Note 1: σ is standard deviation

Note 2: Tables usually use: 90% Level = 1.65 Standard Deviation
95% Level = 1.96 Standard Deviation
99% Level = 2.58 Standard Deviation

mal distribution is completely determined by its two parameters: mean and standard deviation. A normal distribution is visualized in Figure 7.6.

Fortunately, it is not necessary to perform cumbersome calculations to determine optimum sample size. Tables shown in Workshop 2 in this chapter provide, with 95 percent and 99 percent levels of confidence, the sample-size requirements at various levels of response and within acceptable limits of error.

The formulas for calculating sample size—as well as error limits, when results are known from a given sample size—also appear in Workshop 2. These formulas can be useful to you when determining a proper sample size for expected response rates beyond the limits of the table, or for confidence levels other than 95 percent and 99 percent.

WORKSHOP 1

Structuring and Evaluating an Experiment

In order to use an experiment to make an adequate decision, a direct marketer must—

- Sample a population
- Measure relevant variables (often one at a time)
- Compute statistics using these measurements
- Infer something about the probability distributions that exist in the population
- Make a decision mindful of the chance of incurring either a Type I error (when the decision maker rejects the "null" hypothesis even though it is true) or a Type II error (when the decision maker accepts the "null" hypothesis when it is *not* true).

Assume that your own organization wants to test a new promotional strategy against its present strategy, which will be offered to the control group in the experiment. Past experience indicates that a 2 percent response rate can be expected from the present promotion.

Here is a framework for implementation of the experiment:

1. State the hypothesis

2. Develop *a priori* assumptions; compute sample size

3. Structure and perform the test experiment

4. Develop *a posteriori* statistics; judge test validity

5. Make the decision

1. State the Hypothesis

When you test a hypothesis, you are deciding whether an assumption, stated in advance of an experiment, is valid. The null hypothesis (H_0) is generally stated in negative terms and is contrasted to an alternative hypothesis (H_a). In this case, the null hypothesis is structured as—

H_0: *Direct-mail response from the test promotion is equal to or less than direct-mail response from the control promotion.*

Although it is not necessary to state an alternative hypothesis at this stage, doing so implies that one wants the response rate from the test promotion to be *better* than that from the control. The alternative hypothesis, then, is:

H_a: *Direct-mail response from the test promotion is more than direct-mail response from the control promotion.*

2. Develop A Priori Assumptions and Compute Sample Size

A response rate of 2 percent from the control group is the first of three assumptions made prior to conducting the experiment.

The second assumption is of the significance level. Some test results are more significant than others. Because of this, statisticians associate the term *significant* with a specific probability denoted by the Greek letter *alpha* (α), which is decided on *prior* to testing the hypothesis. If $\alpha = .05$ is acceptable, this means that a 95 percent confidence level is acceptable. (The confidence level is equal to 1.00 minus α.) In other words, the test result must diverge far enough from the control result, in the manner stated in the hypothesis, so that such a result could occur with a probability of 0.05 or less if the hypothesis were true. Stated positively, 95 times out of 100 the test result could be expected to be *better*, within *limits*.

The third assumption relates to the limit of error, or the acceptable variance around the mean, i.e., the predicted response rate. This acceptable variance is here assumed to be 15 percent.

Having established these three assumptions, one can either access the 95 percent confidence table or use the formula given in Workshop 2, at the end of this chapter, to calculate the size of the sample. The assumptions and resulting sample size determination are summarized in Figure 7.7. It shows that if a randomly-drawn group of 8,365 were mailed an offer expected to generate 2 percent response, then 95 times out of 100, the response rate would fall in the range of 2 percent ± 15 percent of 2 percent. A response rate below 2.3 percent and above 1.7 percent would be the "same as" 2 percent.

FIGURE 7.7

A priori assumptions and sample size determination.

Expected (Assumed) Response Rate: 2%, 20/M pieces mailed.
Significance Level (α): .05
Confidence Level (1.0 – α): 95%
Limits of Error:

Percent	Response/M Pieces Mailed
+15%	20/M + 3/M = 23/M (2.3%)
–15%	20/M – 3/M = 17/M (1.7%)

Sample Size: 8,365 Pieces to be Mailed

3. Structure and Perform the Test

Having determined an objective sample size of 8,365 pieces to be mailed for the test promotion and a comparable group for the control promotion, the next step is to draw the two groups from a target mailing list which contains 170,000 prospects. Since 8,365 times two equals about 17,000, 10 percent of the total list of 170,000 is drawn. First, a random number between 1 and 10—let's say 8—is selected. Starting with the 8th name in the list, every 10th name is selected: 8, 18, 28, 38, and so on. As names are drawn, they are alternately assigned to the test group and to the control group.

When the promotion is ready, both the test group and the control group are mailed simultaneously. Use a promotion scheduling form to assure proper mailing and to evaluate test results. The form should include—

- A general description of the test and its purpose
- Special production and fulfillment instructions
- List(s) and/or segments mailed
- Printed or broadcast components of the promotion
- Product and offer
- Mailing date
- Sample sizes and how drawn
- Control and test costs

- Responses expected or required for break-even
- Prior tests (if any)
- Key coding
- Considerations pertinent to evaluation of the analysis.

An example of a scheduling form is shown in Figure 7.8

4. Develop A Posteriori Analysis and Test Validity

When results of the experiment are final, or at some statistically projectable point, the response rates from both the test and control groups are evaluated. One evaluation procedure for determining if an observed difference is or is not *statistically significant* is a chi-square (χ^2) test. It is computed from the observed results and compared with a table that lists probabilities for a theoretical sampling distribution. The formula used for such computation and a chi-square (χ^2) distribution table are provided in Workshop 3, at the end of this chapter.

Other statistical techniques used for measuring significant differences include ANOVA (Analysis of Variance, or the *F-test*), the *T-test* (for sample sizes through 30, rarely applicable to direct mail) and the *Z-test* (for sample sizes larger than 30).

Many times *a posteriori* analysis will involve advanced multivariate analytical tools, the subject of the next chapter. While these sound complicated, they can help you reduce the results of your test into easy to grasp, actionable conclusions.

A posteriori analysis is essential in that it faces the rigors of statistics and the tests of significance. But results cannot adequately be analyzed unless there is a record of these results for all segments of the experiment. An example of a form that can help track results on a day-to-day or week-to-week basis is shown in Figure 7.9.

Tracking is facilitated by the use of a *key code* on each response device. Response received by mail can be tracked through a number on the order form. The source of telephone orders can be identified if trained communicators ask for the source identification key code printed on the label of a catalog or other mailed promotion. Broadcast promotion responses can be coded to a unique 800 telephone number, possibly even cross-referenced to a ZIP code for geographic location. Or, telephone respondents can ask to speak to a department or an individual.

FIGURE 7.8
An example of a test scheduling form.

☐ STANDARD OR ☐ TEST OF ☐ PRODUCT ☐ MARKET ☐ PRESENTATION

REPORT NO. _____ REPORT DATE _____

LIST	STATE OR SEGMENT	JOB NO.	TYPE	MAILING DATE	ORIGINATED BY	DATE ORIGINATED

GENERAL INFORMATION

PRODUCT AND OFFER

STANDARD COSTS _____ per M | SALES EXPECTED _____ per M

TEST COSTS

PURPOSE

SALES REQUIRED ON TEST

SPECIAL INSTRUCTIONS

PRIOR TESTS
☐ NO ☐ YES—EXPLAIN

☐ STANDARD ANALYSIS
☐ OTHER—EXPLAIN

☐ APPROVED
☐ DISAPPROVED

SIGNATURE

MAILING COMPONENTS

TEST NO.	DESCRIPTION OF TEST	KEY NO.	QUANTITY	O.S. ENV.	ORDER FORM	LETTER	RETURN ENVELOPE	CIRCULAR	OTHER	OTHER

SUPPLIES

	FORM NUMBER	QUANTITY ORDERED	DATE AVAILABLE

FIGURE 7.9

An example of a form for tracking results.

DATE RELEASED						STATE		KEY					
TEST #	KIND OF TEST					REMARKS							
MAKE UP OF OFFER	O. S. ENV.	LETTER	ORDER FORM		RET. ENV.	CIRCULAR	INSERT	COPY #					

WEEK ENDING			# MAILINGS		$ VOLUME			# SALES			# UNITS			# CONVERSIONS		
#	MO	DAY	CURRENT	TO DATE	CURRENT	TO DATE	P/M	CURRENT	TO DATE	P/M	WK	#	CUM	CURRENT	TO DATE	P/M
1											1					
2											2					
3											3					
4											4					
5											5					
6											6					
7											7					
8											8					
9											9					
10											10					
11											11					
12											12					
13											13					
14											14					
15											15					
16											16					
17											17					
18											18					
19											19					
20											20					
21											21					
22											22					
23											23					
24											24					
25											25					
26											26					

5. Make the Decision

Finally, one makes a decision to accept or to reject the test promotion.

While there can be subjective considerations—relative costs, repetitiveness of an offer, suitability—the decision must be basically an objective one, not influenced by personal preferences, author of the copy, or even a higher authority.

WORKSHOP 2

How to Calculate Sample Size

The size of a sample drawn from a population (list)—e.g., the number of observations in an experiment or test—needs to be carefully calculated in order to assure the validity of the results. Sample sizes can be established by quickly referring to the charts or by following the formula in this workshop.

Let's first define the four statistics—*confidence level, limit of error, expected (or actual) response rate and sample size*—which enter into the calculation:

- *Confidence Level:* The number of times in 100 attempts that the resultant prediction must be correct. The degree of confidence is expressed in terms of number of standard deviations. The number of standard deviations refers to the area covered under a normal curve as shown in Figure 7.6.

- *Limit of Error:* The number of percentage points by which the researcher is allowed to miscalculate the actual response rate. A 20 percent limit of error, assuming a 1 percent response rate, for example, could result in a range of actual response as low as 0.8 percent to as high as 1.2 percent; or, 1% ± 20% of 1%.

- *Expected (Actual) Response Rate:* The number of times, in percentage, that response has or is expected to occur.

- *Sample Size:* The number of observations in the experiment, or test. This is, for example, the number of pieces mailed in a test from which is to be determined the response.

The formula for determining sample size is:

$$N = \frac{(R)\ (1-R)\ (C)^2}{E^2}$$

where:

R is the frequency of response, the response rate, a percentage expressed as a decimal

1 – R is the frequency of nonresponse, also a percentage expressed as a decimal

C is the confidence level, expressed as a number of standard deviations

E is the limit of error expressed as a decimal; and

N is the sample size, the number of pieces to be mailed.

To illustrate the use of the above formula, one can determine the sample size required to be mailed as a test when the expected response rate is 1%; the desired limit of error is ± 0.2%; at a confidence level of 95%. Thus:

$$R = 1\% \ldots 0.01, \text{ expressed as a decimal}$$
$$1 - R = 99\% \ldots 0.99, \text{ expressed as a decimal}$$
$$C = 1.96 \text{ standard deviations, at a 95\% confidence level}$$
$$E = 0.2\% \ldots 0.002, \text{ expressed as a decimal}$$
$$N = \text{to be determined}$$

Substituting the above values into the formula for the determination of sample size, provides this solution:

$$N = \frac{(0.01)\,(0.99)\,(1.96)^2}{(0.002)^2}$$

$$= \frac{(0.01)\,(0.99)\,(3.8416)}{0.000004}$$

$$= \frac{0.03803184}{0.000004}$$

$$= 9{,}508 \text{ pieces to be mailed}$$

Suppose that, having proceeded with the experiment and having mailed 9,508 pieces as a test (with another 9,508 pieces as a control), the *actual* response from the test segment turned out to be 1.5% rather than the *anticipated* 1%? Still at a 95% confidence level, what would be the *limit of error* for continuation mailings projected from this experiment? Here is the formula for determining that:

$$E = \sqrt{(R)(1{-}R)\,/\,N} * C$$

Substituting into this formula the *actual* response rate of 1.5%, with the same notation as before, here is the calculation for limit of error:

$$E = \sqrt{(0.015)(0.985) / 9508} * 1.96$$

$$E = \sqrt{0.000001554} * 1.96$$

$$E = 0.00124 * 1.96$$

$$E = 0.00243 \ldots \text{ or, } 0.243\% \text{ limit of error}$$

These two examples illustrate the statistical importance of setting up direct-mail tests in a manner to assure a sample size adequate for meaningful projection of response rates within acceptable tolerances, i.e., limits of error.

Additionally, they demonstrate the need for accurate determination of the limit of error, the variance that could occur by chance alone, not as a result of significant differences in particular direct marketing efforts.

When predicting the response rate from a market segment, after testing, one must recognize "error by chance." In the calculation above, in which actual test response was 1.5% and error limit was calculated to be ± 0.243%, any response rate from continuation mailings to this market segment within the range of 1.257% and 1.743% would be statistically "same as" the 1.5% prediction. Such variation could have occurred by statistical chance alone.

Note, too, that a ± 0.243 variance is 16% of a response rate of 1.5% whereas a ± 0.2 variance is 20% of a lower response rate of 1%. This demonstrates that the relative amount of variance decreases as the response rate increases. Variance also decreases as sample size increases.

Decreasing error limits or increasing confidence levels both increase the sample-size requirement. Thus, there is a trade-off between the cost of additional mailing pieces and the value of the precision of information derived from a test.

Fortunately, it is not usually necessary to perform cumbersome calculations like these. Tables for 95 percent and 99 percent confidence levels, for response rates up to 4 percent and limits of error up to 70 percent, are provided in Figures 7.10 and 7.11.

FIGURE 7.10

Sample sizes for response rates between 0.1% and 4.0%. Confidence level of 95%.

R (Response)	Limits of Error (Expressed as Percentage Points) .02	.04	.06	.08	.10	.12	.14	.16	.18	.20	.30	.40	.50	.60	.70
.1	95,929	23,982	10,659	5,995	3,837	2,665	1,957	1,499	1,184	959	426	240	153	106	78
.2	191,666	47,916	21,296	11,979	7,667	5,324	3,911	2,994	2,366	1,917	852	479	307	213	156
.3	287,211	71,803	31,912	17,951	11,488	7,978	5,861	4,487	3,546	2,872	1,276	718	459	319	234
.4	382,564	95,641	42,507	23,910	15,303	10,627	7,807	5,977	4,723	3,826	1,700	956	612	425	312
.5	477,724	119,431	53,080	29,858	19,109	13,270	9,749	7,464	5,987	4,777	2,123	1,194	764	530	390
.6	572,693	143,173	63,632	35,793	22,908	15,908	11,687	8,948	7,070	5,727	2,545	1,432	916	636	467
.7	667,470	166,867	74,163	41,717	26,699	18,541	13,622	10,429	8,240	6,675	2,966	1,669	1,068	741	545
.8	762,054	190,514	84,673	47,628	30,482	21,168	15,552	11,907	9,408	7,621	3,387	1,905	1,219	847	622
.9	856,447	214,112	95,160	53,528	34,258	23,790	17,478	13,382	10,573	8,564	3,806	2,141	1,370	951	699
1.0	950,648	237,662	105,628	59,415	38,026	26,407	19,401	14,854	11,736	9,506	4,225	2,376	1,521	1,056	776
1.1	1,044,656	261,164	116,072	65,291	41,786	29,018	21,319	16,322	12,897	10,446	4,643	2,611	1,671	1,160	853
1.2	1,138,472	284,618	126,496	71,155	45,539	31,624	23,234	17,788	14,055	11,385	5,060	2,846	1,821	1,265	929
1.3	1,232,097	308,024	136,899	77,006	49,284	34,225	25,145	19,251	15,211	12,321	5,476	3,080	1,971	1,369	1,006
1.4	1,325,529	331,382	147,280	82,845	53,021	36,820	27,051	20,711	16,364	13,255	5,891	3,314	2,121	1,473	1,082
1.5	1,418,769	354,692	157,640	88,673	56,751	39,410	28,954	22,168	17,515	14,188	6,305	3,547	2,270	1,576	1,158
1.6	1,511,818	377,954	167,980	94,489	60,473	41,995	30,853	23,622	18,664	15,118	6,719	3,780	2,419	1,680	1,234
1.7	1,604,674	401,168	178,297	100,292	64,187	44,574	32,748	25,073	19,811	16,047	7,132	4,012	2,567	1,783	1,310
1.8	1,697,338	424,334	188,592	106,083	67,894	47,148	34,639	26,521	20,955	16,973	7,543	4,243	2,716	1,886	1,385
1.9	1,789,810	447,452	198,868	111,863	71,592	49,717	36,526	27,966	22,096	17,898	7,955	4,474	2,863	1,988	1,461
2.0	1,882,090	470,523	209,121	117,631	75,284	52,280	38,410	29,407	23,235	18,821	8,365	4,705	3,011	2,091	1,536
2.1	1,974,178	493,544	219,352	123,386	78,967	54,838	40,289	30,846	24,372	19,742	8,774	4,935	3,158	2,193	1,611
2.2	2,066,074	516,518	229,564	129,129	82,643	57,391	42,165	32,282	25,507	20,661	9,182	5,165	3,306	2,295	1,686
2.3	2,157,778	539,444	239,753	134,861	86,311	59,938	44,036	33,715	26,638	21,578	9,590	5,394	3,452	2,397	1,761
2.4	2,249,290	562,322	249,920	140,581	89,972	62,480	45,903	35,145	27,769	22,493	9,997	5,623	3,599	2,499	1,836
2.5	2,340,609	585,152	260,068	146,288	93,624	65,017	47,767	36,572	28,896	23,406	10,403	5,851	3,745	2,600	1,911
2.6	2,431,737	607,934	270,192	151,983	97,269	67,547	49,627	37,996	30,021	24,317	10,807	6,079	3,891	2,702	1,985
2.7	2,522,673	630,668	280,296	157,667	100,907	70,074	51,483	39,416	31,144	25,227	11,211	6,307	4,036	2,803	2,059
2.8	2,613,416	653,354	290,380	163,339	104,537	72,595	53,335	40,834	32,264	26,134	11,615	6,534	4,181	2,904	2,133
2.9	2,703,968	675,992	300,440	168,998	108,159	75,110	55,183	42,249	33,382	27,039	12,017	6,760	4,326	3,004	2,207
3.0	2,794,328	698,582	310,480	174,645	111,773	77,620	57,026	43,661	34,497	27,943	12,419	6,986	4,471	3,105	2,281
3.1	2,884,495	721,124	320,499	180,281	115,380	80,125	58,867	45,070	35,611	28,845	12,820	7,211	4,615	3,205	2,355
3.2	2,974,470	743,618	330,496	185,904	118,979	82,623	60,702	46,476	36,721	29,745	13,220	7,436	4,759	3,305	2,428
3.3	3,064,254	766,254	340,471	191,516	122,570	85,118	62,535	47,878	37,850	30,642	13,619	7,660	4,903	3,404	2,501
3.4	3,153,845	788,461	350,427	197,115	126,154	87,607	64,364	49,278	38,936	31,538	14,017	7,884	5,046	3,504	2,574
3.5	3,243,244	810,811	360,360	202,703	129,730	90,089	66,188	50,675	40,040	32,432	14,414	8,108	5,189	3,603	2,647
3.6	3,332,452	833,113	370,271	208,278	133,298	92,568	68,009	52,069	41,141	33,325	14,811	8,331	5,332	3,702	2,720
3.7	3,421,467	855,367	380,163	213,842	136,859	95,041	69,825	53,460	42,240	34,214	15,207	8,554	5,474	3,801	2,793
3.8	3,510,290	877,572	390,031	219,393	140,412	97,507	71,638	54,848	43,336	35,103	15,601	8,776	5,616	3,900	2,865
3.9	3,598,921	899,730	399,878	224,932	143,957	99,969	73,446	56,233	44,430	35,989	15,995	8,997	5,758	3,998	2,938
4.0	3,687,360	921,840	409,706	230,460	147,494	102,426	75,252	57,615	45,522	36,874	16,388	9,218	5,900	4,097	3,010

Source: John E. McNichols, Alan Drey Company, Inc. Chicago, IL

FIGURE 7.11

Sample sizes for response rates between 0.1% and 4.0%. Confidence level of 99%.

R (Response)	Limits of Error (Expressed as Percentage Points)														
	.02	.04	.06	.08	.10	.12	.14	.16	.18	.20	.30	.40	.50	.60	.70
.1	165,709	41,427	18,412	10,357	6,628	4,603	3,381	2,589	2,046	1,657	736	414	265	184	135
.2	331,087	82,772	36,787	20,693	13,243	9,197	6,756	5,173	4,087	3,311	1,471	827	529	368	270
.3	496,132	124,033	55,126	31,008	19,845	13,781	10,125	7,752	6,125	4,961	2,205	1,240	794	551	405
.4	660,846	165,212	73,427	41,303	26,434	18,356	13,486	10,325	8,158	6,608	2,937	1,652	1,057	734	539
.5	825,228	206,307	91,692	51,577	33,009	22,923	16,841	12,894	10,187	8,252	3,667	2,063	1,320	916	673
.6	989,279	247,320	109,919	61,380	39,571	27,480	20,189	15,457	12,213	9,893	4,396	2,473	1,582	1,099	807
.7	1,152,997	288,249	128,111	72,062	46,120	32,027	23,530	18,015	14,234	11,530	5,124	2,882	1,845	1,281	941
.8	1,316,384	329,096	146,265	82,274	52,655	36,565	26,864	20,569	16,251	13,164	5,850	3,291	2,106	1,462	1,074
.9	1,479,439	369,859	164,381	92,465	59,178	41,095	30,192	23,116	18,264	14,794	6,575	3,698	2,367	1,643	1,208
1.0	1,642,163	410,541	182,463	102,635	65,687	45,616	33,513	25,658	20,273	16,422	7,299	4,105	2,627	1,825	1,340
1.1	1,804,554	451,138	200,505	112,784	72,182	50,126	36,827	28,195	22,278	18,045	8,020	4,511	2,887	2,004	1,473
1.2	1,966,614	491,654	218,512	122,913	78,665	54,628	40,134	30,728	24,279	19,666	8,740	4,917	3,146	2,185	1,605
1.3	2,128,342	532,085	236,482	133,021	85,134	59,121	43,435	33,255	26,275	21,283	9,459	5,321	3,405	2,365	1,737
1.4	2,289,739	572,435	254,414	143,108	91,590	63,603	46,729	35,777	28,268	22,897	10,176	5,724	3,663	2,544	1,869
1.5	2,450,803	612,700	272,310	153,175	98,032	68,077	50,016	38,293	30,256	24,508	10,892	6,127	3,921	2,723	2,000
1.6	2,611,536	652,884	290,170	163,221	104,461	72,542	53,296	40,805	32,241	26,115	11,607	6,529	4,178	2,901	2,132
1.7	2,771,937	692,984	307,992	173,246	110,877	76,997	56,569	43,311	34,221	27,719	12,319	6,930	4,435	3,079	2,263
1.8	2,932,007	733,002	325,777	183,250	117,280	81,444	59,836	45,812	36,197	29,320	13,030	7,330	4,691	3,257	2,393
1.9	3,091,744	772,936	343,527	193,234	123,670	85,881	63,096	48,308	38,169	30,917	13,741	7,729	4,946	3,435	2,523
2.0	3,251,150	812,788	361,238	203,197	130,046	90,309	66,350	50,799	40,137	32,512	14,449	8,128	5,202	3,612	2,654
2.1	3,410,224	852,556	378,912	213,139	136,409	94,728	69,596	53,284	42,100	34,102	15,156	8,525	5,456	3,789	2,783
2.2	3,568,967	892,242	396,551	223,060	142,759	99,138	72,836	55,765	44,061	35,690	15,862	8,922	5,710	3,965	2,913
2.3	3,727,377	931,844	414,152	232,961	149,095	103,537	76,068	58,239	46,016	37,273	16,566	9,318	5,964	4,141	3,042
2.4	3,885,456	971,364	431,716	242,841	155,418	107,929	79,294	60,710	47,968	38,855	17,268	9,714	6,216	4,317	3,172
2.5	4,043,203	1,010,800	449,245	252,700	161,728	112,311	82,513	63,174	49,915	40,432	17,970	10,108	6,469	4,492	3,300
2.6	4,200,619	1,050,155	466,734	262,538	168,025	116,682	85,726	65,634	51,859	42,006	18,669	10,501	6,721	4,667	3,429
2.7	4,357,702	1,089,425	484,187	272,356	174,308	121,046	88,932	68,088	53,798	43,577	19,367	10,894	6,972	4,842	3,557
2.8	4,514,454	1,128,614	501,606	282,153	180,578	125,402	92,131	70,538	55,734	45,145	20,064	11,286	7,223	5,016	3,685
2.9	4,670,874	1,167,718	518,984	291,929	186,835	129,745	95,324	72,982	57,664	46,708	20,759	11,677	7,473	5,189	3,812
3.0	4,826,963	1,206,741	536,327	301,685	193,079	134,081	98,508	75,421	59,591	48,270	21,453	12,067	7,723	5,363	3,940
3.1	4,982,719	1,245,679	553,635	311,420	199,309	138,409	101,687	77,854	61,514	49,827	22,145	12,457	7,972	5,536	4,067
3.2	5,138,144	1,284,536	570,903	321,134	205,526	142,725	104,858	80,284	63,433	51,381	22,836	12,845	8,221	5,709	4,194
3.3	5,293,237	1,323,309	588,135	330,827	211,729	147,034	108,024	82,706	65,348	52,932	23,525	13,233	8,469	5,881	4,321
3.4	5,447,999	1,362,000	605,333	340,500	217,920	151,333	111,183	85,124	67,258	54,480	24,213	13,620	8,716	6,053	4,447
3.5	5,602,428	1,400,607	622,490	350,152	224,097	155,621	114,334	87,537	69,165	56,024	24,899	14,006	8,964	6,224	4,573
3.6	5,756,526	1,439,132	639,611	359,783	230,261	159,903	117,479	89,945	71,067	57,565	25,584	14,391	9,210	6,395	4,699
3.7	5,910,292	1,477,573	656,699	369,393	236,412	164,174	120,616	92,347	72,966	59,103	26,268	14,775	9,456	6,567	4,842
3.8	6,063,727	1,515,932	673,746	378,983	242,549	168,435	123,749	94,745	74,860	60,637	26,949	15,159	9,702	6,737	4,949
3.9	6,216,829	1,554,207	690,756	388,552	248,673	172,688	126,872	97,137	76,750	62,168	27,629	15,542	9,947	6,907	5,074
4.0	6,369,600	1,592,400	707,733	398,100	254,784	176,933	129,991	99,525	78,636	63,696	28,309	15,924	10,191	7,077	5,199

Source: John E. McNichols, Alan Drey Company, Inc. Chicago, IL

WORKSHOP 3

How to Measure Differences

Assume that a sample has been properly selected and is of an adequate size. Assume further that an experiment has been designed and implemented in a valid manner. It now remains for the direct marketer to be able to recognize the *difference* in the response rate from a test and that from a control, with some degree of confidence and within an acceptable limit of error.

When evaluating the results of an experiment, one needs to know if a difference is *statistically significant*. The chi-square (χ^2) test may be used for validating such a difference. The null hypothesis offered is that there is, in fact, no difference between the response from the test and that from the control. A statistic (χ^2) is computed from the observed results and this is compared with a table that lists probabilities for a theoretical sampling distribution. A chi-square distribution table appears in Figure 7.12.

A χ^2 distribution varies according to the number of degrees of freedom, defined as the number of observations allowed to vary. The number of degrees of freedom is determined by multiplying the number of observations in rows (minus 1) times the number of observations in columns (minus 1) thus: $(r - 1)(c - 1)$, where r is the number of rows and c is the number of columns.

The contingency table below, called a 2-by-2, involves just one degree of freedom: $(2 - 1)(2 - 1) = 1$. A table of this form can be used for evaluating the significance of the difference between the response rate from a test and that from a control:

	Test	*Control*	*Totals*
Response	A	C	A + C
Nonresponse	B	D	B + D
Total mailed	A + B	C + D	A + B + C + D = N

The statistic χ^2 is computed as follows:

$$\chi^2 = \frac{N\,(|AD - BC| - N/2)^2}{(A+B)(C+D)(A+C)(B+D)}$$

Here is a sample calculation:

	Test	Control	Totals
Response	200	100	300
Nonresponse	800	900	1700
Total mailed	1000	1000	2000

$$\chi^2 = \frac{2,000 \times [180,000 - 80,000 - 1,000]^2}{1,000 \times 1,000 \times 300 \times 1,700}$$

$\chi^2 = 38.4$, which is significant at the 99++% level since it exceeds the value in the χ^2 table for one degree of freedom for a significance level of 0.001, given as 10.83

FIGURE 7.12

Critical values of chi-square (χ^2).

df — Probability under H_0 that $\chi^2 \geq$ Chi-Square

df	.99	.98	.95	.90	.80	.70	.50	.30	.20	.10	.05	.02	.01	.001
1	.00016	.00063	.0039	.016	.064	.15	.46	1.07	1.64	2.71	3.84	5.41	6.64	10.83
2	.02	.04	.10	.21	.45	.71	1.39	2.41	3.22	4.60	5.99	7.82	9.21	13.82
3	.12	.18	.35	.58	1.00	1.42	2.37	3.66	4.64	6.25	7.82	9.84	11.34	16.27
4	.30	.43	.71	1.06	1.65	2.20	3.36	4.88	5.99	7.78	9.49	11.67	13.28	18.46
5	.55	.75	1.14	1.61	2.34	3.00	4.35	6.06	7.29	9.24	11.07	13.39	15.09	20.52
6	.87	1.13	1.64	2.20	3.07	3.83	5.35	7.23	8.56	10.64	12.59	15.03	16.81	22.46
7	1.24	1.56	2.17	2.83	3.82	4.67	6.35	8.38	9.80	12.02	14.07	16.62	18.48	24.32
8	1.65	2.03	2.73	3.49	4.59	5.53	7.34	9.52	11.03	13.36	15.51	18.17	20.09	26.12
9	2.09	2.53	3.32	4.17	5.38	6.39	8.34	10.66	12.24	14.68	16.92	19.68	21.67	27.88
10	2.56	3.06	3.94	4.86	6.18	7.27	9.34	11.78	13.44	15.99	18.31	21.16	23.21	29.59
11	3.05	3.61	4.58	5.58	6.99	8.15	10.34	12.90	14.63	17.28	19.68	22.62	24.72	31.26
12	3.57	4.18	5.23	6.30	7.81	9.03	11.34	14.01	15.81	18.55	21.03	24.05	26.22	32.91
13	4.11	4.76	5.89	7.04	8.63	9.93	12.34	15.12	16.98	19.81	22.36	25.47	27.69	34.53
14	4.66	5.37	6.57	7.79	9.47	10.82	13.34	16.22	18.15	21.06	23.68	26.87	29.14	36.12
15	5.23	5.98	7.26	8.55	10.31	11.72	14.34	17.32	19.31	22.31	25.00	28.26	30.58	37.70
16	5.81	6.61	7.96	9.31	11.15	12.62	15.34	18.42	20.46	23.54	26.30	29.63	32.00	39.29
17	6.41	7.26	8.67	10.08	12.00	13.53	16.34	19.51	21.62	24.77	27.59	31.00	33.41	40.75
18	7.02	7.91	9.39	10.86	12.86	14.44	17.34	20.60	22.76	25.99	28.87	32.35	34.80	42.31
19	7.63	8.57	10.12	11.65	13.72	15.35	18.34	21.69	23.90	27.20	30.14	33.69	36.19	43.82
20	8.26	9.24	10.85	12.44	14.58	16.27	19.34	22.78	25.04	28.41	31.41	35.02	37.57	45.32
21	8.90	9.92	11.59	13.24	15.44	17.18	20.34	23.86	26.17	29.62	32.67	36.34	38.93	46.80
22	9.54	10.60	12.34	14.04	16.31	18.10	21.24	24.94	27.30	30.81	33.92	37.66	40.29	48.27
23	10.20	11.29	13.09	14.85	17.19	19.02	22.34	26.02	28.43	32.01	35.17	38.97	41.64	49.73
24	10.86	11.99	13.85	15.66	18.06	19.94	23.34	27.10	29.55	33.20	36.42	40.27	42.98	51.18
25	11.52	12.70	14.61	16.47	18.94	20.87	24.34	28.17	30.68	34.38	37.65	41.57	44.31	52.62
26	12.20	13.41	15.38	17.29	19.82	21.79	25.34	29.25	31.80	35.56	38.88	42.86	45.64	54.05
27	12.88	14.12	16.15	18.11	20.70	22.72	26.34	30.32	32.91	36.74	40.11	44.14	46.96	55.48
28	13.56	14.85	16.93	18.94	21.59	23.65	27.34	31.39	34.03	37.92	41.34	45.42	48.28	56.89
29	14.26	15.57	17.71	19.77	22.48	24.58	28.34	32.46	35.14	39.09	42.56	46.69	49.59	58.30
30	14.95	16.31	18.49	20.60	23.36	25.51	29.34	33.53	36.25	40.26	43.77	47.96	50.89	59.70

Source: George Kress, *Marketing Research*. Reston, VA: Reston Publishing Co., Inc., 1979, p. 351.

8

What You Need to Know about Advanced Multivariate Analysis

Surveys and experiments are a rich source of lessons for the direct marketer. But before you can apply the results to future promotional efforts, you need to analyze the observations generated by tests and research.

Four advanced statistical tools used for measurement and evaluation of research and analysis have demonstrated particular relevance for direct marketing:

1. Regression and correlation analysis

2. Discriminant analysis

3. Factor analysis

4. Cluster analysis.

These tools can help direct marketing decision makers evaluate test results, profile individual customers within market segments and observe differences between respondents and nonrespondents in order to calculate the probability of response from a particular market segment or promotion effort.

Typically, direct marketers are conditioned to test only one independent variable at a time. Yet, a dependent variable such as response rate is often influenced by the interaction of *many* independent variables, including demographic makeup of a market segment or economic indicators at the time of a promotion. Some of these can be controlled by the experimenter; others cannot be.

Multivariate analysis can help analyze results when many variables are at work—especially the always unpredictable human factor. These tools can help you analyze multiple variables and reduce them to a manageable number.

Regression and Correlation Analysis

Statistically oriented economists use regression and correlation analysis to describe economic activity in terms of national income and gross national product. Recently, more and more direct marketers have been using this statistical tool to predict marketing effectiveness.

Regression and correlation analysis can bring data about one or more independent variables together in order to predict the value of a dependent variable. For instance, through correlation analysis one can develop a possible relationship between the results from a direct-mail solicitation (the dependent variable) and the length of the letter containing the direct-mailed offer (an independent variable).

If the values of both the independent variable(s) and the dependent variable move upward together, the correlation is positive. If one increases when the other decreases, the correlation is negative. Highly correlated variables (positive or negative) are then entered into regression analysis, from which the extent of correlation can be verified.

Correlation between independent and dependent variables is measured by a coefficient which is stated in a decimal form ranging from 0 to 1 (for positive correlation) and from 0 to –1 (for negative correlation). Positive or negative, a coefficient of 1 indicates a perfect correlation and "0" indicates none.

In general, regression and correlation analysis is a statistical tool for finding and describing a functional relationship between a dependent variable, such as sales, and the independent variables influencing sales, such as the characteristics of buyers. This is done by fitting a line to observed points depicting relationships in such a way as to minimize the sum of the squares of the differences between these observed points (actual sales) and the estimated points (predicted sales) as determined by the regression line. Hence, the process is sometimes called "least squares."

When one independent variable is used, the statistical tool is termed *simple* regression; when more than one such variable is used, it is termed *multivariate* regression. In reality, the relationship is not always linear; more than likely, in direct marketing analysis, the relationship will be curvilinear. That is, sales response might increase at an accelerating rate relative to the rate of change of the causal variable(s).

The general form of a linear regression equation is:

$$Y = a + bX_1 + cX_2 + dX_3 \ldots + nX_n$$

where:

X = some independent variable (age of respondent, price, offer)

a = a constant that brings the scale of X into the scale of Y

b = some slope of straight line relationship of X and Y

Y = the dependent variable (response rate to a promotion offer)

There is a degree of uncertainty or randomness associated with the regression equation in that every prediction involves some error. The larger the uncertainty, the more the potential for error in prediction.

An example of a simple (one variable) regression and correlation analysis process is shown in this illustration:

- Response rate to a direct mail effort (Y) is to be evaluated relative to the educational level (X_1) of ZIP code areas in which prospects and respondents reside.

- The measured response rate from ZIP code areas in which the educational level of residents 26+ years of age averages 6 years of schooling is 1/M pieces mailed; the response rate from those areas where the average is 8 years of schooling is 3/M; the response rate from those areas averaging 10 years of schooling is 8/M; from 12 years, it is also 8/M; from 14 years, it is 13/M; and the response rate from those ZIP code areas averaging 16 years of schooling is 15/M pieces mailed.

- A regression line is mathematically fitted among these six points on an *X/Y* chart, as shown in Figure 8.1, so that the sum of the distances between the actual response rates and those estimated from the regression prediction line, squared in order to eliminate negative numbers below the line, is as small as possible.

- In terms of the regression formula, the beginning intercept a, near the bottom of a vertical Y axis measuring response rates, represents the amount of response that would occur regardless of educational level. The coefficient b determines the slope of the regression line measured as rise/run (movement of response rate on a vertical Y axis divided by movement of educational level on a horizontal X axis). The dependent variable Y, measured on the vertical axis, is the response per thousand pieces of direct mail sent. The independent variable X_1, measured on the horizontal axis, is the educational level of ZIP code areas mailed.

FIGURE 8.1

Regression and correlation analysis—"fitting a line" to the observed relationship between response to a promotion effort (Y), the dependent variable, and the educational level of ZIP code areas of respondents (X₁), the independent variable.

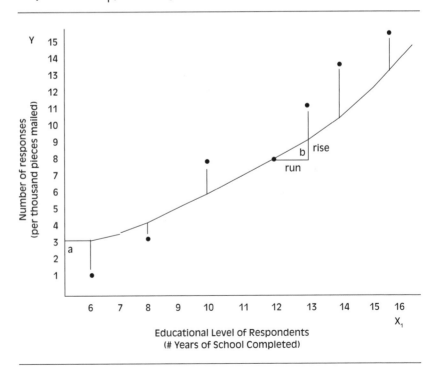

- Since the data results in an upward-sloping line which shows accelerating upward movement, we observe a *positive* correlation; response rate increases as educational level increases. If the response rate were to decrease as educational level increases, a distinct possibility in certain cases, correlation is *negative.*

  This illustration involves just one independent variable and is termed simple regression and correlation analysis. When two or more variables are involved, the process is termed multivariate and each variable enters the regression calculation in rank ordering of correlation with the dependent variable, in a manner termed *stepwise.* As many as 25 or more independent variables could interact with each other in the process of stepwise multivariate regression and correlation analysis.

  In such multivariate analysis, it is not uncommon to find both positive and negative correlation among the variables used. In a stepwise procedure involving a large number of independent variables, it also sometimes happens that a variable will enter the regression and later be removed as the calculation proceeds. Only the absolutely smallest number of variables will result when such a process is completed. This involves the principle of *parsimony,* meaning that the regression analysis will seek the *minimum* number of variables required for optimum explanation.

  In seeking, through regression and correlation analysis, a summary of relationships of independent variables to a dependent variable, the researcher must be concerned with how valid the prediction will be. The element of error is associated with the distance from the actual observed points to the points on the prediction line.

  This error is shown by the *coefficient of correlation* and is described by the statistic R. Squaring this derived value, to R^2, provides the *coefficient of determination.* An R value of 0.70 (which some consider to be a minimum acceptable statistic in the use of regression analysis in direct marketing) provides an R^2 value of 0.49. This means that 49 percent of the observed difference in response rate is associated with, explained by, the independent variable(s) correlated with the dependent response rate variable.

  The b constant is the *coefficient of regression.* It determines the slope of the regression line. Depending on whether this coefficient is positive or negative, the regression line can slope upward or downward. This line shows the amount of change in the dependent variable, *Y*, which is associated with the change in one (or more) independent variable(s), *X*.

Discriminant Analysis

Discriminant analysis has its roots in anthropology and medicine. Through measurement of cholesterol level, blood pressure, smoking habits, exercise regime and other attributes, a physician is able to predict the probability that a person will suffer a heart attack. The anthropologist can, through measurement and analysis, calculate the probability that a particular bone might have come from a particular species.

Likewise, the direct marketer can use discriminant analysis to predict potential interest in a particular product by analyzing the demographic and lifestyle characteristics of those who have already purchased the product.

Discriminant analysis is not intended to predict the *value* of a dependent variable, as is regression analysis. Rather, it is concerned with *whether or not an event will occur.* Discriminant analysis endeavors to predict the probability of occurrence of an event, such as the likelihood—but not the level—of response to a direct-mail solicitation.

For example, *Reader's Digest* used discriminant analysis to discover the characteristics that are likely to indicate *Reader's Digest* readers. The magazine applied nineteen independent variables to a sample of known readers and known nonreaders. Analysis of these variables revealed that those more likely to be readers included families with older male heads; fewer female children under 6 years of age; husbands who were blue-collar workers; families which had lived in fewer houses and cases where the respondent perceived himself as being "friendly" on a personality scale.

By pinpointing distinctions between readers and nonreaders, discriminant analysis facilitated the *Reader's Digest*'s search for market segments and prospect mailing lists that matched these reader characteristics.

Factor Analysis

Direct marketing organizations can accumulate a great deal of information about their customers. To be truly useful, however, there must be an integrated approach to retrieving and using this valuable information.

Factor analysis can help by reducing large data into understandable, smaller pieces of information. It combines a large number of data variables into *factors* that convey statistically all the essential information of the original set of variables, but result in fewer, recognizable factors than there were original variables. Because factor analysis can identify a *latent* fundamental relationship creating communality among these factors, it can also point out relationships among the variables that may otherwise be difficult to see.

Ultimately, this statistical tool can be used to group the characteristics of lifestyles, media, emotional stimuli, price levels or products. For example, it might group a hundred or more demographic variables describing the residents of a particular ZIP code area into a manageable number of factor definitions such as "Rural Residers," "Senior Citizens," or "Affluent Lifestyle." (Sometimes groups are bestowed more imaginative names, like "Golden Pond," "Shotguns and Pickups," or "Furs and Station Wagons.")

The statistical process of a factor analysis involves the reading of a correlation matrix by the computer, which looks for patterns of high inter-correlation among the variables. It then proceeds to take linear combinations of the variables so that the information and the correlation is reduced to a smaller number of variables. After principal components are extracted, these are rotated (analytically) from their beginning position in order to simplify interpretation of the factors. These variables are then regressed against each *factor loading* and the resultant regression coefficients are used to generate *factor scores*.

A "Senior Citizen" factor might contain high values for all of these demographic variables simultaneously: age, widowed, retired, tenure of residence, age of housing structure, foreign-born. There might also be negative correlation with family size.

An "Affluent Lifestyle" factor might contain high values for these variables: income, education, home value, number of cars owned, presence of automatic dishwashers. There might also be negative correlation with federal poverty level indicators.

As with any statistical tool, factor analysis poses problems of reliability and validity. It is incumbent on the user of factor analysis to show that the resultant factors are not simply artifacts of the chosen sample but relate in some way to actual, observable behavior.

Cluster Analysis

Cluster analysis also groups variables, characteristics, actions, persons, or objects into natural aggregations. While factor analysis can group variables, characteristics, or survey question responses into common elements called *factors,* cluster analysis is a means of grouping persons or objects having the same underlying traits into common elements called *clusters.*

Using the "Rural Residers," "Senior Citizens," or "Affluent Lifestyle" variables identified by factor analysis, cluster analysis can group tens of thousands of ZIP code areas into clusters displaying a commonality of occurrence of these factors.

One major reason for this clustering is to achieve a statistically significant sample size. The clustering of comparable ZIP code areas is necessary because it is rare for the number of pieces mailed into a single 5-digit ZIP area to be of an adequate number for valid measurement.

Cluster analysis is of two types: *teardown* and *buildup.* An example of the teardown variety is TREE analysis, a technique which breaks a total population into subgroups. One of the best known of the TREE techniques is AID (automatic interaction detector). A recent variation is CHAID, which injects a chi-square measurement of observed differences.

Direct marketers use the AID/CHAID statistical tools, which require discrete input of independent variables, to identify an infinite number of subgroups (cells) of a total mailing list according to response rates. Like the branches of a tree, evolving into smaller offshoot branches, AID/CHAID analysis proceeds to break a total population into consecutively smaller subgroups in this manner: total population > females only > ages 25–45 only > married only > with small children only > working only > college graduates only > living in the midwest only. Response rates are then evaluated within each consecutive cell.

The second type of cluster analysis, the buildup variety, constructs groupings depending on how similar an entity (ZIP code area, person, object) is to another entity. From a total population, groups of entities are constructed through the addition of one entity at a time to each group, based on how similar an entity is to another entity, or to the average of a group of entities already formed.

This form of cluster analysis is sometimes referred to as *Q factor analysis* in that it examines similarities in the characteristics of individuals or else the average of all persons in an entity such as a ZIP code area. It can then be used to create clusters of either individuals or ZIP code areas depending on how similar each entity is to each other entity.

CASE STUDY

Benefiting from Multivariate Analysis

A travel company that offers package tours through mail order to older persons desires to increase its marketing effectiveness. It seeks to do this through segmentation of its marketplace within the state of Florida using demographic independent variables in addition to age. It constructs a prediction model utilizing three of the multivariate statistical tools discussed in this chapter: regression and correlation analysis, cluster analysis, and factor analysis.

The firm has developed, from census and proprietary data sources, a total of 103 demographic variables describing each of 35,000 geographic ZIP code areas. These variables are expressed as either averages or frequency distributions. The 103 variables, describing 27 characteristics of each ZIP code area, are shown in Figure 8.2.

Several of these variables have been normalized—that is, they have been indexed to some larger area such as a Sectional Center (the first three digits of a five-digit code) or a state (such as Mississippi vs. New York) in order to achieve environmental, as opposed to absolute, measurement.

This means that the *relative* income level in a rural Mississippi ZIP code area is compared with the *relative* income level of an urban area in New York City rather than in *absolute* dollars. A "high" dollar income level in the rural Mississippi area could be relatively "low" in urban New York City.

Variables have also been subjected to factor analysis in order to discover the typical lifestyle factors and the associated independent variables. These are shown in Figure 8.3.

The *dependent* variable is market penetration, defined in this instance as the *response rate* (total responses divided by the total number of pieces mailed) to the travel company's direct-mail offer of package tours to the older residents of Florida.

To maximize the number of observations and assure statistical validity of both measurement and prediction, the response rate is calculated within *clusters* of ZIP code areas which have common characteristics—produced, of course, using cluster analysis. Ultimately, these clusters will be described as market segments in which penetration levels can be correlated with their characteris-

FIGURE 8.2

A listing of 27 characteristics and 103 variables describing 35,000 ZIP code areas.

Characteristic	Variable Description	Characteristic	Variable Description
Type of Area	% Urban % Rural Non-Farm % Rural Farm	*Industry of* *Work Force*	% Construction % Manufacturing % Transportation % Communication
Race	% White % Black % Indian % Japanese % Chinese % Filipino % Spanish American % Other		% Wholesale/Retail % Finance % Professional % Educational % Public Administration % Other
		Family Size	Average Family Size
Nativity	% Native/Native Parents % Native/Foreign Parents % Foreign Born	*Poverty*	% Individual Below Poverty % Family Below Poverty
		Mobility	% Moved Past 2 Years
Origin of *Foreign Born*	% United Kingdom % Ireland % Sweden	*Home Ownership*	% Owner-Occupied
	% Germany % Poland	*Home/Rent Value*	Median Value of Owned Median Rent Paid
	% Czechoslovakia % Austria % Hungary	*Age of Structure*	Median Structure Age
	% Russia % Italy	*Tenure of Residence*	Median Tenure of Resid.
	% Canada % Mexico	*Income*	Median Indiv. Income Median Family Income
	% Cuba % Other	*Conspicuous* *Consumption*	Mean Current Auto Value
Mother Tongue	% English % German	*Dwelling Size*	Median Owner-Occupied Median Renter-Occupied
	% Polish % Yiddish % Italian % Spanish % All Others % Not Reported	*Dwelling Type*	% Single Family Dwellings % 2-Unit Structures % 3/4-Unit Structures % 5/49-Unit Structures % 50+-Unit Structures % Mobile Homes/Trailers
Marital Status	% Married % Widowed % Divorced % Separated % Never Married	*Household* *Equipment*	% With Washer % With Dryer % With Dishwasher % With Freezer % With Television
Age	Median Age		% With UHF-TV % With Battery Radio
Education	Median Education Level		
Occupation of *Work Force*	% Professional/Technical % Farm Manager	*Structure* *Equipment*	% With Air Conditioning % With Multi-Bath % With Central Heat % With Public Water % With Public Sewer
	% Managerial % Clerical % Sales		
	% Craftspeople % Operatives	*Kitchen*	% Lacking Kitchen
	% Service % Farm Laborer	*Direct Access*	% Lacking Direct Access
	% Other Laborer % Armed Services	*Telephone*	% Having Telephone
	% Unemployed	*Autos Registered*	% With One Auto % With Two Autos % With Three+ Autos

FIGURE 8.3

Typical lifestyle factors with associated variables.

FACTOR 1:	*AFFLUENCE*	
	Education:	16+ years of school completed
		13-15 years of school completed
	Occupation:	manager, official, proprietor
		professional, technical, sales
	Industry:	finance
	Value/Owner-occupied:	$100,000+
	Rent Paid/Renter:	$600+
	Structure Equipment:	Multibath
	Household Equipment:	Dishwasher
	Average Auto Value:	High
	Family Income:	$50,000+
	Individual Income:	$30,000+
FACTOR 2:	*SETTLED SINGLES*	
	Household Relation:	primary individual or non-relative
		of the head of the household
	Marital Status:	divorced
	Housing Occupancy:	renter
	Dwelling Type:	multiple family unit
	Dwelling Size:	1/2-room owner-occupied
		1/2-room renter-occupied
	Auto Registration:	one auto
FACTOR 3:	*POVERTY*	
	Education:	1-8 years school completed
	Kitchen:	lacking kitchen
	Telephone:	lacking telephone
	Value/Owner-occupied:	under $10,000
	Rent Paid/Renter:	under $100
	Poverty:	individuals below poverty level
		families below poverty level
	Family Income:	under $14,000
	Individual Income:	under $5,000
FACTOR 4:	*SENIOR CITIZEN*	
	Nativity:	native born of foreign parents
	Country of Origin:	eastern Europe
	Age:	65+
		50-64
	Marital Status:	widowed
	Structure Age:	50+ years
	Tenure of Residence:	35+ years
FACTOR 5:	*RURAL RESIDER*	
	Type of Area:	rural farm
	Occupation:	farmer, farm manager, farm laborer
	Industry:	other

tics. At this stage, both *environmental* (indexed) measurement and *interaction* among the variables defining clusters are important considerations.

Calculation of penetration is simple. Within each cluster of ZIP code areas, the response rate is calculated as shown here:

ZIP Code Area Clusters	Total No. of Pieces Mailed	Total No. of Responses	% Responses/ Mailed
A	5,793	60	1.04
B	2,735	33	1.21
C	6,731	136	2.02
D	4,341	119	2.74

From this table, it is readily apparent that there is an increasing rate of response from A to B, from B to C, and from C to D. These differences can be explained by evaluating the independent variables entering in and deemed significant through regression analysis shown in Figure 8.4, which enables the transfer of these findings from a sample to the total population without first having mailed that total population.

The derived linear regression equation (of the form given in this chapter: $Y = a + bX$) becomes a formula for predicting estimated response rates from ZIP code area clusters not yet solicited but having similar characteristics to those sampled.

Correlation analysis by the travel company identifies the strength of the relationship between cluster response rates (the dependent variable) and each of the 103 selected demographics (independent variables).

Figure 8.4 reproduces a condensed printout of the stepwise multivariate regression analysis that follows the correlation analysis. From an availability of 27 independent variables, each a surrogate of a demographic characteristic of ZIP code areas, ten steps are taken and eight variables remain at the conclusion of Step 10. The reference numbers of these eight variables, together with their simple correlation coefficients, are shown at the bottom of Figure 8.4.

The resulting R^2 value of 0.803748 (the multiple coefficient of determination) indicates that 80% of the variance in response is explained by presence or absence of these eight variables.

The derived regression equation enables a rank ordering of predicted response rates attributable to each five-digit ZIP code area within each cluster. This is visualized in Figure 8.5.

FIGURE 8.4

Stepwise multivariate regression analysis.

```
STEP # 1
    VARIABLE ENTERING              X– 5
R = 0.583959          R SQ. = 0.341008
    F LEVEL =            23.8036
    STANDARD ERROR OF Y =      0.06341
    CONSTANT TERM =        0.27470726
```

VARIABLE NO.	COEFFICIENT	STD ERR OF COEFF
X– 5	–0.28683022E–01	0.00594

```
STEP #  2
    VARIABLE ENTERING              X– 2
R = 0.717396          R SQ. = 0.514658
    F LEVEL =            16.1004
    STANDARD ERROR OF Y =      0.05504
    CONSTANT TERM =        0.25037676
```

VARIABLE NO.	COEFFICIENT	STD ERR OF COEFF
X– 2	0.11710477	0.02951
X– 5	–0.25006641E–01	0.00524

```
STEP #  3
    VARIABLE ENTERING              X– 16
R = 0.814453          R SQ. = 0.663334
    F LEVEL =            19.4310
    STANDARD ERROR OF Y =      0.04637
    CONSTANT TERM =        0.17120540
```

VARIABLE NO.	COEFFICIENT	STD ERR OF COEFF
X– 2	0.12946498	0.02503
X– 5	–0.21160301E–01	0.00450
X– 16	0.10500204E–01	0.00241

```
STEP #  4
    VARIABLE ENTERING              X– 14
R = 0.831825          R SQ. = 0.691934
    F LEVEL =            3.9919
    STANDARD ERROR OF Y =      0.04488
    CONSTANT TERM =        0.11676645
```

VARIABLE NO.	COEFFICIENT	STD ERR OF COEFF
X– 2	0. 12659431	0.02427
X– 5	–0.18140811E–01	0.00462
X– 14	0.27103789E–01	0.01373
X– 16	0.99606328E–02	0.00235

FIGURE 8.4 (Continued)

```
STEP # 10
     VARIABLE ENTERING                 X- 22
R = 0.896520              R SQ. = 0.803748
     F LEVEL =            2.8542
     STANDARD ERROR OF Y =      0.03766
     CONSTANT TERM =            0.39812356
```

VARIABLE NO.	COEFFICIENT	STD ERR OF COEFF
X- 2	0.13928533	0.02095
X- 9	-0.20301903E-02	0.00064
X- 10	-0.87198131E-02	0.00257
X- 14	0.69082797E-01	0.01875
X- 15	0.13623666E-01	0.00421
X- 16	0.22368859E-01	0.00380
X- 22	-0.15226589E-02	0.00091
X- 23	-0.21373443E-02	0.00081

Figure 8.5 shows the highest to the lowest, as well as the cumulative, predicted penetration percentages (response rates). It also shows both individual and cumulative base mailing list counts for each ZIP code area within each cluster. Note the variance of the *actual* response rate, shown for each ZIP code area in the third column, attributable to the small number mailed in each area.

Figure 8.5 reveals that, from a total mailing quantity of 1,277,262 pieces, the overall average response rate is predicted to be 1.95 percent. The response rate from the top cluster (#39) is predicted at 4.49 percent; that from the bottom cluster (#30) is predicted at 0.76 percent. The ratio, top vs. bottom, is very nearly 1:6. Note, too, that the response rate from the top cluster is 2.3 times the overall average of 1.95 percent; that from the bottom is 39 percent.

To attain an average response of 2.55 percent (which is 31 percent better than the overall average), the company should stop after cluster #10 with marginal response of 2.06 percent and mail only 511,276 pieces.

Or, limiting mailing quantity to 242,935 pieces, about 20 percent of the list availability, average response would be 2.87 percent, an improvement of 47 percent over the 1.95 percent overall average.

From this analysis, the company decides how big a market segment is needed, then predicts what overall response rate will be.

FIGURE 8.5

Rank ordering of ZIP code area clusters according to response rate predicted by regression analysis.

Cluster #	ZIP #	Penetration Actual	Percentages Pred	Cum Pred	Base Counts ZIP Only	Cumulative
39	32009	.00	.0449	.0449	89	89
	32265	.00	.0449	.0449	4	93
	32560	.1070	.0449	.0449	93	186
	32563	.00	.0449	.0449	6	192
	32710	.00	.0449	.0449	37	229
	32732	.00	.0449	.0449	200	429
	32740	.00	.0449	.0449	42	471
	32766	.1500	.0449	.0449	200	671
	33070	.0460	.0449	.0449	651	1322
	33470	.00	.0449	.0449	132	1454
	33527	.00	.0449	.0449	716	2170
	33534	.0590	.0449	.0449	505	2675
	33550	.00	.0449	.0449	194	2869
	33556	.0750	.0449	.0449	528	3397
	33569	.0480	.0449	.0449	1637	5034
	33584	.0390	.0449	.0449	1001	6035
	33586	.00	.0449	.0449	62	6097
	33592	.0770	.0449	.0449	518	6615
	33600	.0750	.0449	.0449	398	7013
	33943	.00	.0449	.0449	139	7152
3	32600	.0420	.0342	.0363	28855	36007
11	32301	.0560	.0327	.0360	3533	39540
	32304	.0230	.0327	.0358	2532	42072
	32500	.0360	.0327	.0355	4873	46945
	32570	.0120	.0327	.0354	2312	49257
	32601	.0330	.0327	.0350	7826	57083
	33030	.0120	.0327	.0348	5564	62647
13	32211	.0240	.0246	.0291	6134	222185
	32303	.0160	.0246	.0290	4243	226428
	32561	.0330	.0246	.0289	1203	227631
	32701	.0140	.0246	.0289	2038	229669
	32751	.0140	.0246	.0288	3379	233048
	32786	.00	.0246	.0288	229	233277
	32789	.0170	.0246	.0287	7543	240820
	33511	.0370	.0246	.0287	2115	242935
10	33900	.0210	.0206	.0255	53503	511276
37	33062	.0170	.0111	.0198	6834	1234153
	33140	.00	.0111	.0198	56	1234209
	33154	.0060	.0111	.0198	3120	1237329
	33160	.0130	.0111	.0197	16354	1253683
	33306	.0100	.0111	.0197	986	1254669
30	33064	.0210	.0076	.0196	8201	1262870
	33516	.00	.0076	.0195	11202	1274072
	33570	.0090	.0076	.0195	3190	1277262

Or, it sets its minimum response rate requirement (average or marginal), then, determines how many pieces it can mail.

At this point, of primary importance to the travel company is a description of the profiles which exist in Florida. Just what influence might each of these exert on the response rate to a travel tour offer directed to older persons? Factor analysis produces these three explanatory lifestyle profiles which are present in clusters with high response rates:

- *Rural Residers*—Variables *positively* associated with this factor include rural farm and rural non-farm types of areas; farm manager and farm laborer occupations; housing is often in mobile homes and trailers; housing is equipped with food freezers but often lacks formal kitchens; ancestry is East European. *Negatively* associated variables are access to public water and public sewers; finance industry; multi-family dwelling units.

- *Social Class*—"*Lower half*" variables *positively* associated with this factor include occupation as laborers, operatives, service workers, unemployed; poverty levels; divorced, separated, and widowed marital status; older housing; longer tenure of residence. "*Upper half*" variables, *negatively* associated, are high housing value; housing equipped with amenities such as air conditioning and dishwashers; 2 or more autos; high income; high education levels; occupations in management, sales, professional, technical; finance industry.

- *Ancestry/Heritage*—Variables with *positive* association are native-born with English as a mother tongue; foreign-born with countries of origin including the United Kingdom, Canada, Ireland, Austria, and Germany; housing in owner-occupied single-family units. *Negatively* associated variables include foreign born; immigrated from Cuba; Spanish is mother tongue; multiple family rental housing.

Because the overall response to this offer is double the break-even requirement for the acquisition of new customers, the travel company decides to validate its research. Six months after the first offer, the entire list is remailed, rank-ordered in quintiles of response as predicted from regression analysis.

As expected, the overall response drops to about half that of the first effort. What is important, however, is that the relationship (response rate indices) of the quintiles are virtually the same for both efforts, as detailed in this table:

Rank Ordered Quintile	Number of Pieces Mailed	First Effort Response %	First Effort Index	Second Effort Response %	Second Effort Index
1	242,935	2.87	147%	1.36	143%
2	268,341	2.26	116%	1.08	111%
3	230,592	1.94	99%	0.96	99%
4	290,001	1.54	79%	0.81	84%
5	245,393	1.19	61%	0.67	67%

9

How to Segment a Market Using a Database

The market segmentation techniques, research and testing methods, and statistical tools presented in the previous three chapters are not merely academic theories. Applied to a database, they can help a company determine *exactly* where its customers and prospects are to be found. This chapter shows how a hypothetical company used all of these tools and techniques to sharpen its promotional strategies and boost its bottom line.

Computer Software and Hardware, "CSH" for short, is a hypothetical company that produces and/or provides a variety of product lines: personal, mid-range, and mainframe computers; storage devices; and networking, operating, and applications software.

Distribution of CSH products is multi-channel. Its primary channel is through computer dealers, discount retailers and full-service department stores. It sells and services these middlemen through its own salesforce, which also calls on selected organizations who purchase direct from CSH. Direct-response advertising is used to create retail traffic for its intermediaries as well as to generate leads for its own salesforce. For small businesses and certain consumer households, a mail-order catalog, CSH Direct, is employed.

Since CSH sells in both consumer *and* industrial markets, its direct marketing embraces both business-to-business and business-to-consumer activities. Its database includes those who buy direct from it, as well as those who buy from resellers. These buyers return warranty and registration information direct to CSH. Salespersons provide information, too. Transactions are recorded.

Enhancements provided from outside sources include determination of gender, ethnicity, and credit worthiness.

In order to acquire new customers, CSH has invested heavily in compiling a profile of its present customers. Its first step was to look at its demographic characteristics. Consumer variables are shown in Figure 9.1. Figure 9.2 shows the demographics of industrial customers. In both illustrations, the frequency of occurrence of a characteristic, such as age (for consumers) or years in business (for firms) is shown in a banded table as a percentage.

To refine its customer profile, CSH examined the transaction history of its customers. Figure 9.3 shows how CSH identified customers according to their transaction history. Records derived from its database indicate that 38.09 percent of first purchases were for personal computers. Among those whose first purchase was hardware, only 18.73 percent of second purchases were of personal computers. By contrast, among customers first purchasing software, 41.13 percent of second purchases were for personal computers.

By analyzing these trends, CSH learned to direct its on-going promotion only to customers most likely to be interested in what is being offered. Customers whose first purchase was of hardware products received follow-up promotions for applications software; software purchasers were offered hardware.

CSH also found the source of on-going purchases to be an important consideration. Figure 9.3 indicates that personal follow-ups by the CSH sales force were more productive in generating second purchases. Direct mail leads were more productive for qualifying first-time buyers.

Further analysis of the CSH customer database provides the good news shown in Figure 9.4:

1. Customer attrition declines over time

2. Frequency of purchases increases over time

3. Average revenue per purchase increases as customers remain active.

This information will become input for later calculation of the lifetime value of their customers (LTV), to be discussed in Chapter 12. As you will see, LTV analysis enables you to direct customer acquisition efforts to those who have the most long-range potential in terms of persistency and amount of purchase.

FIGURE 9.1
Consumer market demographic variables.

Demographics:	#	%
By Title:		
Mr.	383,615	73.81%
Mrs.	46,443	8.94%
Ms.	81,317	15.65%
Miss	4,975	0.96%
Dr.	3,390	0.65%
	519,740	100.00%
By Gender:		
Female	132,735	25.54%
Male	387,005	74.46%
	519,740	100.00%
By Age Band:		
65-plus	80,121	15.42%
50–64	124,196	23.90%
35–49	182,766	35.16%
34-minus	132,657	25.52%
	519,740	100.00%

(Continued)

FIGURE 9.1 (Continued)

Demographics:	#	%
By Gender/HoH/Marital Status:		
Male/HoH/Not Married	138,765	26.70%
Male/HoH/Married	154,955	29.81%
Male/HoH/Other	93,285	17.95%
Female/HoH/Not Married	38,992	7.50%
Female/Married	84,279	16.22%
Female/Other	9,464	1.82%
	519,740	100.00%

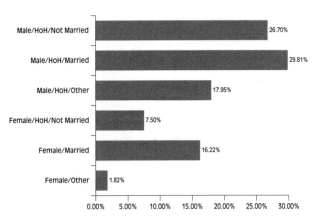

By Primary Ethnic Code:		
English	151,703	29.19%
French	24,505	4.71%
German	46,571	8.96%
Hebrew	25,128	4.83%
Irish	51,234	9.86%
Italian	25,390	4.89%
Scottish	16,802	3.23%
Spanish	16,339	3.14%
Swedish	14,512	2.79%
Welsh	22,845	4.40%
Unknown	124,711	23.99%
	519,740	100.00%

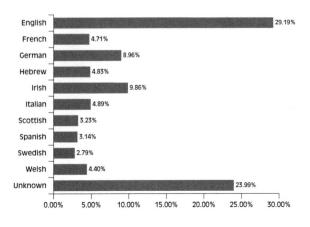

FIGURE 9.2

Industrial market demographic variables.

SIC Code	Description	#	%
1521	General Building Contractors	1,082	4.86%
3900	Manufacturers-Miscellaneous	1,233	5.54%
4000	Transportation/Communications/Public Utilities	911	4.09%
5081	Wholesale-Commercial Machine & Equipment	1,169	5.25%
5311	Department Stores	1,130	5.07%
5943	Office Supply Stores	256	1.15%
5961	Mail Order Houses	195	0.88%
5999	Computer Stores	577	2.59%
6000	Finance/Insurance/Real Estate	1,308	5.87%
7011	Hotels & Motels	749	3.36%
7311	Advertising Agencies	894	4.01%
7321	Credit Report & Collections	804	3.61%
7331	Direct Mail Advertising	1,480	6.64%
7372	Computer Software Services	1,757	7.89%
7374	Data Processing Services	1,734	7.78%
7379	Computer Related Services	1,779	7.99%
7399	Business Services	1,707	7.66%
8911	Engineering & Architectural Services	1,732	7.78%
8931	Accounting, Audit, and Bookkeeping Services	1,777	7.98%
		22,274	100.00%

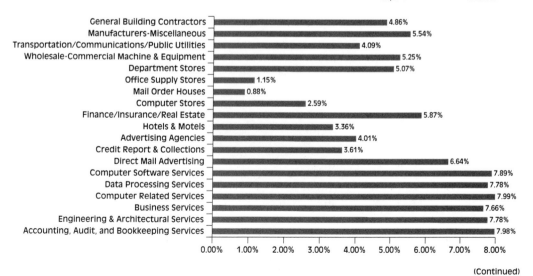

(Continued)

FIGURE 9.2 (Continued)

Years In Business:	#	%
Under 1	2,589	11.62%
1 to 5	8,770	39.37%
6 to 10	7,768	34.87%
Over 10	3,147	14.13%
	22,274	100.00%

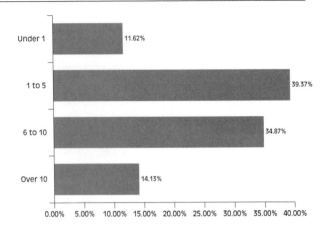

Employees	#	%
1 to 10	8,660	38.88%
11 to 25	5,324	23.90%
26 to 100	4,743	21.29%
101 to 500	2,526	11.34%
501 plus	1,021	4.58%
	22,274	100.00%

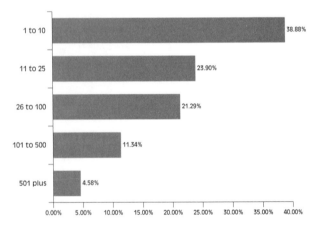

Credit Evaluation	#	%
Not Eval	8,938	40.13%
Good	8,748	39.27%
Reasnabl	2,410	10.82%
Pot'l Risk	877	3.94%
Prob Risk	617	2.77%
Signif Risk	572	2.57%
Seri's Risk	112	0.50%
	22,274	100.00%

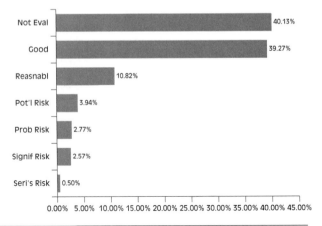

FIGURE 9.3

Market segmentation by product purchased, sequence of purchase, and source of purchase.

Product Lines and Sequencing	All Product Lines Combined		First Purchase from CHS		Second Purchase (First:Hardware)		Of Those Who Did	Second Purchase (First:Software)		Of Those Who Did
	#	%	#	%	#	%	%	#	%	%
Product Line:										
Personal Computers	386,681	32.82%	197,973	38.09%	37,349	14.19%	18.73%	85,243	33.23%	41.13%
Mid-range Computers	171,058	14.52%	27,558	5.30%	19,866	7.55%	9.96%	14,341	5.59%	6.92%
Mainframe Computers	25,712	2.18%	7,718	1.48%	1,034	0.39%	0.52%	109	0.04%	0.05%
Storage Devices	37,949	3.22%	10,491	2.02%	4,453	1.69%	2.23%	2,034	0.79%	0.98%
Networks	32,681	2.77%	19,509	3.75%	9,362	3.56%	4.69%	9,093	3.55%	4.39%
Operating Software	271,058	23.01%	118,213	22.74%	30,809	11.70%	15.45%	19,138	7.46%	9.23%
Application Software	252,949	21.47%	138,278	26.61%	96,536	36.67%	48.41%	77,315	30.14%	37.30%
No Second Purchase	na	na	na	na	63,840	24.25%	na	49,218	19.19%	na
	1,178,088	100.00%	519,740	100.00%	263,249	100.00%	100.00%	256,491	100.00%	100.00%
Source:										
DM Lead	829,054	70.37%	417,874	80.40%	156,377	59.40%	na	169,223	65.98%	na
Mail Order	66,176	5.62%	41,630	8.01%	13,994	5.32%	na	11,348	4.42%	na
Salesperson	282,858	24.01%	60,236	11.59%	92,878	35.28%	na	75,920	29.60%	na
	1,178,088	100.00%	519,740	100.00%	263,249	100.00%	na	256,491	100.00%	na

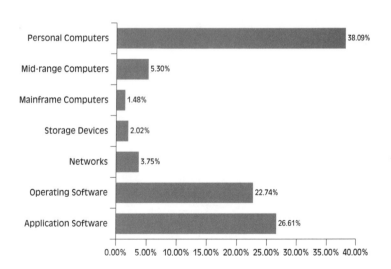

First Purchase by Product Line

(Continued)

FIGURE 9.3 (Continued)

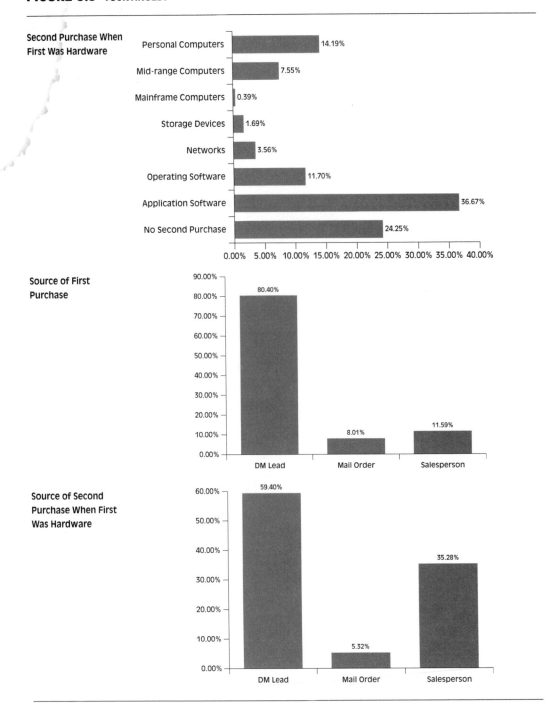

Second Purchase When First Was Hardware

Source of First Purchase

Source of Second Purchase When First Was Hardware

FIGURE 9.4

CSH customer continuity, purchase frequency, and average revenue.

CSH Customer Continuity	1st Purchase	2nd Purchase	3rd Purchase	4th Purchase	5th Purchase	Total 2++
# Customer Purchases	519,740	406,682	335,279	298,151	279,886	1,319,998
% of First Purchase	100.00%	78.25%	64.51%	57.37%	53.85%	253.97%
% of Prior Purchase	100.00%	78.25%	82.44%	88.93%	93.87%	na
Avg. Time-Lapse (Months)	na	14.54	13.77	12.88	12.12	53.31
Avg. Revenue/Purchase	$2,637	$2,746	$2,847	$2,938	$3,033	$11,564

CSH Customer Continuity

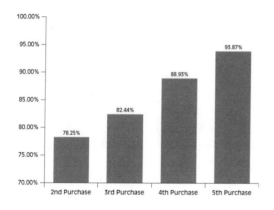

CSH Avg Revenue/Purchase

CSH Customer Frequency

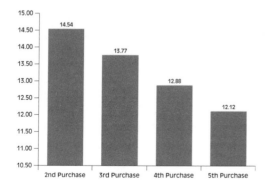

Finally, CSH overlaid demographic and transactional data with environmental data to build profiles of *prospects* most likely to respond to its offers. Figures 9.5 and 9.6 provide the findings of this database market segmentation for CSH's *consumer* market. Figures 9.7 through 9.11 present the findings on its *industrial* market.

CSH Customer Penetration vs. All Households

A key step in profiling CSH customers was determining market penetration within clusters of demographically comparable ZIP code areas. Once these clusters were derived, CSH customers were indexed to all households falling within the clusters. Figure 9.5 records, in a condensed format, the degree of cumulative marketing effectiveness within quintiles (20% groupings) of clusters comprised of about 150 ZIP code areas.

The key measurement, in the last column, is an index derived by dividing the percentage of customers by the percentage of households.

A clear-cut and statistically-reliable pattern emerges from this evaluation. When clusters of ZIP code areas are quintiled in rank-order, the penetration rate of all CSH customers within the top 20 percent of all households is 245.07 percent of the average penetration of all quintiles whereas the bottom 20 percent is 32.77 percent—a ratio of 1:7.48. The top cluster (#76) is 533.41 percent of the average of all clusters; the bottom cluster (#131, not shown) is 19.80 percent of the average —a ratio of 1:27.94.

CSH has also determined that the penetration of its customers, on average, is 50 percent greater in urban ZIP codes than in rural areas. They reason that this is because of local availability of resellers or, possibly, it is because past promotional efforts have been *directed* to urban areas.

Correlation and Regression Analysis

In order to more effectively direct promotional efforts to responsive market segments, CSH used statistical correlation and regression analysis to determine the *reasons why* there are observed differences in customer penetration of market segments.

FIGURE 9.5
CHS customer penetration vs. all households.

Cluster ID	# Cstmrs	% Cstmrs	Cum% Cstmrs	# Hshlds	% Hshlds	Cum% Hshlds	Cstmrs/ Hshlds	Index Cstmrs/Hshlds
76	30,017	5.78%	5.78%	936,715	1.08%	1.08%	3.20%	533.41%
74	18,715	3.60%	9.38%	672,713	0.78%	1.86%	2.78%	463.09%
142	5,153	0.99%	10.37%	200,105	0.23%	2.09%	2.58%	428.65%
23	52,744	10.15%	20.52%	2,057,236	2.38%	4.47%	2.56%	426.77%
34	12,458	2.40%	22.91%	526,053	0.61%	5.08%	2.37%	394.21%
43	11,276	2.17%	25.08%	617,424	0.71%	5.79%	1.83%	304.00%
56	11,489	2.21%	27.29%	858,465	0.99%	6.78%	1.34%	222.77%
62	7,998	1.54%	28.83%	649,998	0.75%	7.53%	1.23%	204.82%
83	13,976	2.69%	31.52%	1,286,248	1.49%	9.02%	1.09%	180.87%
10	11,269	2.17%	33.69%	1,051,051	1.21%	10.24%	1.07%	178.47%
64	3,364	0.65%	34.34%	319,481	0.37%	10.61%	1.05%	175.27%
15	5,850	1.13%	35.46%	581,162	0.67%	11.28%	1.01%	167.56%
136	2,058	0.40%	35.86%	210,228	0.24%	11.52%	0.98%	162.95%
7	9,962	1.92%	37.77%	1,134,881	1.31%	12.83%	0.88%	146.12%
16	6,331	1.22%	38.99%	724,740	0.84%	13.67%	0.87%	145.41%
75	903	0.17%	39.17%	104,413	0.12%	13.79%	0.86%	143.96%
32	12,664	2.44%	41.60%	1,525,454	1.76%	15.55%	0.83%	138.19%
45	7,267	1.40%	43.00%	881,316	1.02%	16.57%	0.82%	137.25%
36	11,318	2.18%	45.18%	1,408,780	1.63%	18.20%	0.80%	133.73%
33	2,970	0.57%	45.75%	404,179	0.47%	18.67%	0.73%	122.32%
Q1 Ttl:	237,782	45.75%		16,150,642	18.67%		1.47%	245.07%
Obsrvn:	20	20		20	20			
Mean:	11,889	2.29%		807,532	0.93%			
Q2 Ttl:	111,688	21.49%	67.24%	18,055,403	20.87%	39.54%	0.62%	102.97%
Obsrvn:	24	24		24	24			
Mean:	4,654	0.90%		752,308	0.87%			
Q3 Ttl:	74,427	14.32%	81.56%	17,108,916	19.78%	59.31%	0.44%	72.41%
Obsrvn:	23	23		23	23			
Mean:	3,236	0.62%		743,866	0.86%			
Q4 Ttl:	61,705	11.87%	93.43%	17,858,600	20.64%	79.96%	0.35%	57.51%
Obsrvn:	37	37		37	37			
Mean:	1,668	0.32%		482,665	0.56%			
Q5 Ttl:	34,138	6.57%	100.00%	17,341,260	20.04%	100.00%	0.20%	32.77%
Obsrvn:	33	33		33	33			
Mean:	1,034	0.20%		525,493	0.61%			
Grand Ttl:	519,740	100.00%		86,514,821	100.00%		0.60%	100.00%
Obsrvn:	137			137				
Mean:	3.794			631,495				

Figure 9.6 presents significant findings from this analysis, which CSH performed to associate demographic variables defining ZIP code area clusters with their own penetration of these clusters.

Variables are indexed and presented as Z-values, a statistical technique for relating the presence or absence of an independent variable within a ZIP code area cluster to a national average of this variable, with indexing above or below that average. Home value, for example, is shown to be above or below the national average rather than high or low in absolute terms. Using Z-values of independent variables as predictors provides uniformity and thus increases reliability of the analysis.

CSH found the demographic profiles of ZIP code area clusters shown in Figure 9.6 to be well defined. The simple correlation coefficients (values between "0" and "1," with the latter being "perfect") of the Z-values of 33 variables show relationships, both positive and negative, between these variables and penetration, which is defined as "Customers ÷ Households." The variable definitions ending with "90" were derived from the 1990 Census. The variables beginning with "SD" are standard deviation (from the mean) values. The variable called AVGHHPCOWND, meaning the average number of households within a cluster owning personal computers, was derived from Simmons data. The variable called AVGCSTMRREV, meaning the average customer revenue within a cluster, was derived from the CSH transactions database.

Multivariate regression analysis of the Z-values of the 33 independent variables, with penetration (Customers ÷ Households) as the dependent variable, provides a comfortable coefficient of correlation: R SQ = 0.878598. This means that 87.86 percent of observed differences in penetration shown in Figure 9.5 can be explained by presence and interaction of the selected variables.

CSH learned from the analysis that penetration is *positively* correlated with these variables:

- Average Home Value

- Male-Headed Households

- Households Owning a PC

- Education Level of Household Head

- SD Rent Paid

- Owner Occupancy

FIGURE 9.6

CSH correlation and regression analysis to associate variables with market penetration.

Simple Correlation Coefficient r Against Y = Cstmrs/Hshlds

Observations = 137;   # Variables = 33

Variable Z	r =	Variable Z	r =	Variable Z	r =
SDHOMEVALU90	0.7113	HOUSINGUNTS90	0.2026	SDAGE90	−0.0399
AVGRENTPAID90	0.7015	#HSHLDS90	0.1892	SEXRATIO90	−0.0424
SDRENTPAID90	0.6949	#POPULATION90	0.1586	HOUSNGUNITS90	−0.0531
AVGHOMEVAL90	0.6832	%OWNEROCC90	0.1276	%HISPANPOP90	−0.0679
SDHHINCOME90	0.6818	%HHMALEHD90	0.1205	%OCCHSNG90	−0.1013
HHEDUCATION90	0.6554	%HSUNTSVAC90	0.1081	%HHFEMHD90	−0.1209
AVGHHINCOM90	0.5251	AVGHSUNTSZ90	0.0983	%RENTEROCC90	−0.1282
HHOCCUPATN90	0.4715	AVGCSTMRREV	0.0382	AVGHHSIZE90	−0.2151
SDHHSIZE90	0.4483	POPDENSITY90	0.0272	SDLNGTHRES90	−0.2311
AVGHHPCOWND	0.2949	%OTHRETHNC90	−0.0175	AVGLNGTRES90	−0.2551
SDHSUNITSIZE90	0.2302	CHGFMPOP9080	−0.0298	AVGAGE90	−0.3457

Results of Regression Analysis:

R = 0.937336   R SQ = 0.878598   F Level = 1.3797   Probability = 0.82157

Overall Significance F = 68.4743   Probability = 1.0000

Standard Error of Y = 0.00113 Cstmrs/Hshlds

Constant Term = 0.345360720530E-02

Variable Z	Coefficient	Std Error of Coeff	T	Probability
SDRENTPAID90	0.215130676E-02	0.00041712	5.158	1.0000
AVGAGE90	−0.747483350E-02	0.00221732	−3.371	0.9990
HHEDUCATION90	0.367138212E-02	0.00030482	12.044	1.0000
%OWNEROCC90	0.114574501E-02	0.00023145	4.950	1.0000
%HHFEMHD90	−0.153616553E-02	0.00033066	−4.646	1.0000
%HHMALEHD90	0.563505590E-03	0.00036595	1.540	0.8738
AVGHOMEVAL90	0.719776989E-02	0.00202720	3.551	0.9995
AVGHHINCOM90	0.104477377E-02	0.00033925	3.080	0.9974
AVGLNGTRES90	−0.220121286E-02	0.00066147	−3.328	0.9988
SDLNGTHRES90	−0.202317190E-02	0.00060380	3.351	0.9989
AVGHHPCOWND	0.498596809E-03	0.00021442	2.325	0.9783
%RENTEROCC90	−0.426860819E-03	0.00027327	−1.562	0.8791

- Household Income.

Penetration is *negatively* correlated with these variables:

- Average Age
- Renter Occupancy
- Average Length of Residence
- SD Length of Residence
- Female-Headed Households.

These variables explain observed differences in customer penetration of markets, and can be used to identify desired ZIP code areas and thus direct market segmentation and guide the creation of advertising.

CSH Customer Penetration vs. Resellers

In Figure 9.5, CSH measured customer penetration vs. all households within ZIP code clusters; in Figure 9.7, CSH looks at customer penetration vs. resellers. To evaluate the sales potential of resellers, it examines the characteristics of these resellers as well as the socioeconomics and demographics of the community in which each business operates.

To do this, it utilizes an industrial market segmentation system called Smart Business Clusters, developed by Ruf Corporation, Olathe, Kansas. Ruf has statistically categorized the total range of businesses into clusters based on:

1. Business characteristics such as standard industrial classifications, number of employees, years in business

2. Location characteristics such as personal and household demographics and lifestyle indicators

3. Economic activity at the business location such as number of businesses, industry patterns, commerce input-output, bank savings, retail sales.

By evaluating these characteristics, CSH can direct reseller acquisition and motivation efforts into those business clusters which

FIGURE 9.7

CSH customer market penetration vs. resellers.

Cluster ID	# Customers	% Customers	Cum % Cstmrs	# Resellers	% Rsllrs	Cum% Rsllrs	Cstmrs/ Rsllrs	Indx Cstmrs/ Rsllrs
22	56,236	10.82%	10.82%	1,382	6.20%	6.20%	40.69	174.39%
33	57,692	11.10%	21.92%	1,647	7.39%	13.60%	35.03	150.12%
36	43,219	8.32%	30.24%	1,278	5.74%	19.34%	33.82	144.93%
Q1 Ttl:	157,147	30.24%		4,307	19.34%		36.49	156.37%
Obsrvn:	3	3		3	3			
Mean:	52,382	10.08%		1,436	6.45%			
29	12,094	2.33%	32.56%	426	1.91%	21.25%	28.39	121.67%
26	15,779	3.04%	35.60%	557	2.50%	23.75%	28.33	121.40%
23	12,548	2.41%	38.01%	459	2.06%	25.81%	27.34	117.16%
17	8,073	1.55%	39.57%	306	1.37%	27.18%	26.38	113.06%
13	2,308	0.44%	40.01%	92	0.41%	27.60%	25.09	107.51%
9	8,419	1.62%	41.63%	339	1.52%	29.12%	24.83	106.43%
20	26,982	5.19%	46.82%	1,137	5.10%	34.22%	23.73	101.70%
16	14,285	2.75%	49.57%	607	2.73%	36.95%	23.53	100.86%
15	13,518	2.60%	52.17%	577	2.59%	39.54%	23.43	100.40%
Q2 Ttl:	114,006	21.94%		4,500	20.20%		25.33	108.57%
Obsrvn:	9	9		3	9			
Mean:	12,667	2.44%		1,500	2.24%			
35	75,159	14.46%	66.63%	3,275	14.70%	54.24%	22.95	98.35%
Q3 Ttl:	75,159	14.46%		3,275	14.70%		22.95	98.35%
Obsrvn:	1	1		1	1			
Mean:	75,159	14.46%		3,275	14.70%			
25	36,163	6.96%	73.59%	1,587	7.12%	61.37%	22.79	97.66%
32	13,865	2.67%	76.26%	631	2.83%	64.20%	21.97	94.17%
37	10,794	2.08%	78.33%	498	2.24%	66.44%	21.67	92.89%
6	1,671	0.32%	78.66%	83	0.37%	66.81%	20.13	86.28%
40	9,501	1.83%	80.48%	495	2.22%	69.03%	19.19	82.26%
30	4,543	0.87%	81.36%	237	1.06%	70.10%	19.17	82.15%
39	2,961	0.57%	81.93%	160	0.72%	70.81%	18.51	79.31%
8	10,322	1.99%	83.91%	582	2.61%	73.43%	17.74	76.01%
10	21,775	4.19%	88.10%	1,308	5.87%	79.30%	16.65	71.34%
Q4 Ttl:	111,595	21.47%		5,581	25.06%		20.00	85.69%
Obsrvn:	9	9		9	9			
Mean:	12,399	2.39%		620	2.78%			
19	3,186	0.61%	88.72%	192	0.86%	80.16%	16.59	71.11%
41	16,972	3.27%	91.98%	1,063	4.77%	84.93%	15.97	68.42%
28	9,851	1.90%	93.88%	646	2.90%	87.83%	15.25	65.35%
21	4,146	0.80%	94.67%	278	1.25%	89.08%	14.91	63.91%
14	3,102	0.60%	95.27%	219	0.98%	90.06%	14.16	60.70%
7	3,822	0.74%	96.01%	298	1.34%	91.40%	12.83	54.97%
38	3,511	0.68%	96.68%	281	1.26%	92.66%	12.49	53.55%
18	9,035	1.74%	98.42%	746	3.35%	96.01%	12.11	51.90%
24	1,183	0.23%	98.65%	100	0.45%	96.46%	11.83	50.70%
11	3,692	0.71%	99.36%	327	1.47%	97.93%	11.29	48.39%
31	1,754	0.34%	99.70%	202	0.91%	98.84%	8.68	37.21%
2	1,579	0.30%	100.00%	259	1.16%	100.00%	6.10	26.13%
Q5 Ttl:	61,833	11.90%		4,611	20.70%		13.41	57.47%
Obsrvn:	12	12		12	12			
Mean:	5,153	0.99%		384	1.73%			
Grand Ttl:	519,740	100.00%		22,274	100.00%		23.33	100.00%
Obsrvn:	34			34				
Mean:	15,286			655				

have a high propensity for sales, or to avoid efforts in those segments which have a low probability for success. It can also devise new promotions to boost store traffic or generate leads for selected resellers.

Placing each of its 519,740 customers and each of its 22,274 resellers into the Ruf Smart Business Clusters results in the rank-ordering by quintiles shown in Figure 9.7. The key measurement, in the last column for each cluster, is an index derived by dividing the percentage of customers by the percentage of resellers. For example, Quintile 1 contains 30.24 percent of all customers within 19.34 percent of all resellers.

When Smart Business Clusters are quintiled in rank order, the penetration rate of all CSH customers within the top 20 percent of all resellers is 156.37 percent of the average penetration of all quintiles whereas the bottom 20 percent is 57.47 percent—a ratio of 1:2.72. The top Smart Business Cluster (#22) is 174.39 percent of the average of all clusters; the bottom cluster (#2) is 26.13 percent of the average—a ratio of 1:6.67.

To determine the reasons behind the differences in reseller effectiveness, CSH derived a statistical profile of its resellers in the industrial market and overlaid that information onto its Smart Business Clusters. Figures 9.8 through 9.11 present the results.

Figure 9.8 presents the business demographic composition of Smart Business Cluster #22, the top-ranked cluster in Figure 9.7. This cluster is above average in sales revenues, employees, businesses, and older firms with fewer than 10 employees. It is below average in sales revenue per business, the number of employees per business and firms having many employees. The cluster is comprised of many smaller businesses.

The census demographic characteristics of locations of businesses in this cluster, shown in Figure 9.9, are above average in population and its density; both female and male householders; divorced, separated, and never-married individuals; renters; occupied housing; black race; housing unit size; number of housing units and number of households. Census demographics which are below average in this cluster include married population; owners of housing; seasonal and vacant housing; families with children; white race and average household size. The cluster is located in densely populated urban areas.

For comparison, CSH analyzes Smart Business Cluster #2, the one at the bottom of the rank ordering. Figure 9.10 presents the business demographics of this cluster. It is apparent that this clus-

FIGURE 9.8
Business demographics of top Smart Business Cluster.

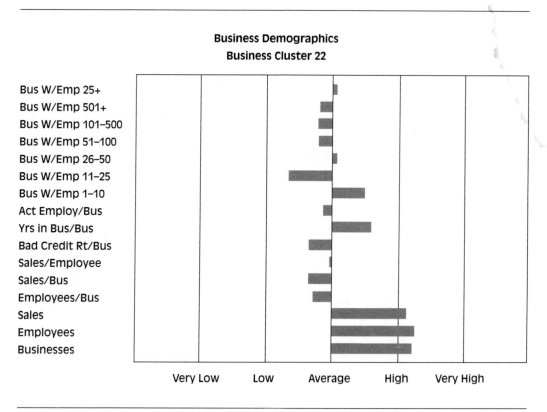

Business Demographics
Business Cluster 22

Source: RUF Corporation.

ter is dominated by relatively few but very large and old businesses with many employees and high average sales. However, the number of businesses and employees as well as sales revenue, in total, are below average. So are businesses with fewer than 10 employees and those with bad credit ratings.

Figure 9.11 visualizes the census demographics of the locations of businesses in this lowest-penetrated cluster. Above-average characteristics are widowed and married population; owner-occupied housing; high average age; and white race. Below-average are population density; male and female householders; divorced, separated, and never married population; families with young children; hispanic and black races; rent and home value; the number of housing units, households and population. This could describe rural and small town areas dominated by a few large firms.

FIGURE 9.9

Census demographics of top Smart Business Cluster.

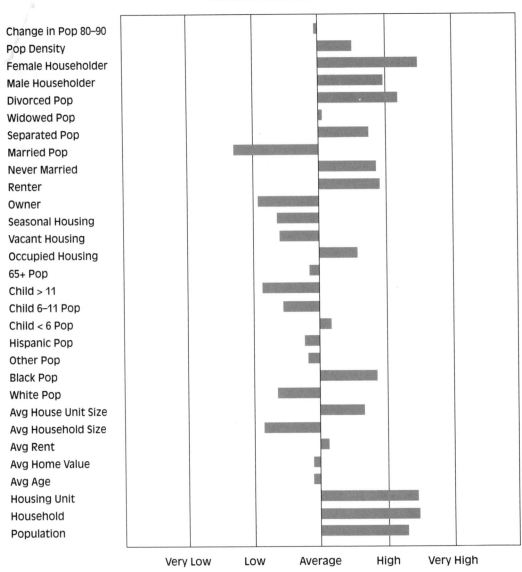

Census Demographics
Business Cluster 22

Source: RUF Corporation.

FIGURE 9.10

Business demographics of bottom Smart Business Cluster.

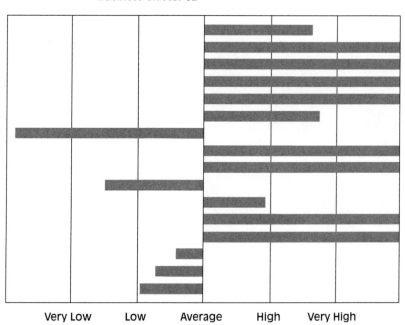

Business Demographics
Business Cluster 02

Categories (top to bottom): Bus W/Emp 25+, Bus W/Emp 501+, Bus W/Emp 101–500, Bus W/Emp 51–100, Bus W/Emp 26–50, Bus W/Emp 11–25, Bus W/Emp 1–10, Act Employ/Bus, Yrs in Bus/Bus, Bad Credit Rt/Bus, Sales/Employee, Sales/Bus, Employees/Bus, Sales, Employees, Businesses

Scale: Very Low, Low, Average, High, Very High

Source: RUF Corporation.

FIGURE 9.11

Census demographics of bottom Smart Business Cluster.

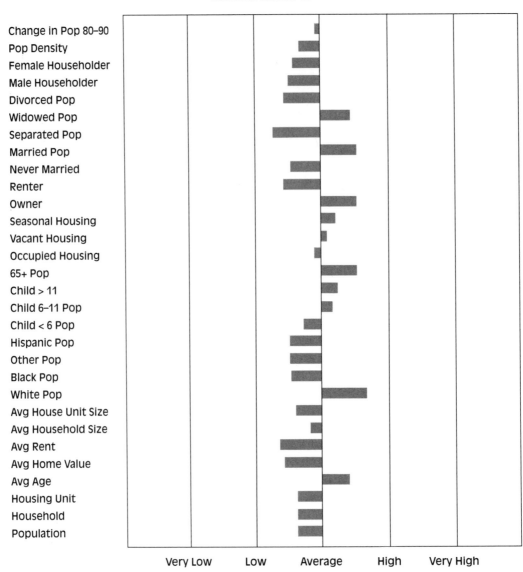

Census Demographics
Business Cluster 02

Conclusion

Database market segmentation helps CSH maximize its *efficiency* and its *effectiveness* in both consumer and industrial markets. By using statistical techniques to discover *who* and *where* its customers and resellers are, CSH can fine-tune its distribution and reselling efforts.

Analyzing this information permits CSH to direct marketing efforts to those who are more likely to be receptive to them—the "rifle shot" of direct marketers. But as this case shows, traditional marketing efforts through resellers and retail channels can also be enhanced by database information and analysis. The extensive profiles of its resellers will enable CSH to—

- Locate optimum markets and resellers

- Increase market penetration in profitable areas

- Increase response to advertising

- Guide sales and salesforce management

- Select optimum retail store locations

- Define penetration and reach of resellers

- Support resellers with lead-generation and traffic-building promotions

The consumer profiles let CSH segment its market and target its direct-response efforts at the most likely customers and prospects. This careful segmentation lets CSH—

- Isolate and profile its best customers

- Provide opportunities for cross-selling, continuity selling, and sales of additional and related products

- Target new customers and direct messages to them

- Make marginal or unprofitable lists pay out

- Make mass compiled lists work

- Selectively mail large response-qualified lists

- Qualify credit

- Develop new products likely to gain acceptance

How a company like CSH can apply this information to its customer acquisition and development activities is the subject of the next section, Part IV: Customers: How to Create and Cultivate Them.

PART
IV

Customers: How to Create and Cultivate Them

Direct marketing begins with information about customers and uses this database to build relationships. And the result of these relationships, if they are successful, is sales.

In Part IV, we will look at how to transform information into a customer relationship through well-thought-out, well-crafted promotions. Starting with what motivates customers to buy, we'll look at how to create offers that your customers want to accept—and promotions that your customers will be pleased to respond to.

We'll show you how companies excel at creating customer relationships through targeted continuity offers and cross-selling efforts—so you can use their models as the starting point for successful customer relationships of your own.

10

Offers + Databases + Promotions = Customers

Promotion—consisting of advertising, selling, publicity, and sales promotion—is a *means,* not an *end.*

In the context of direct marketing, the purpose of promotion is to disseminate information that effects a response. In short, its purpose is to *sell.* Its objective is the creation and cultivation of customers!

The creative process used to develop direct-response promotions in any format or medium begins with *research* and leads to *idea generation* and finally *copywriting.* A successful promotion should have at its heart a concept and an *offer*—a blend of the product, price, and terms—that appeals to the target market.

Customers will respond to offers if these provide benefits that appeal to them. Such benefits are often physical attributes of a product, translated into terms that meet needs. A good *offer* delivers benefits that fulfill needs. Customers don't "buy" quarter-inch drill bits. They "benefit" from fulfilling needs for quarter-inch holes! They don't buy power steering—they buy ease in parking an automobile parallel to a curb.

Direct marketers use promotion techniques that are benefit-oriented. They avoid gimmickry. They rely on facts gathered from a database. They sell *benefits*—and they sell them in a manner that matches a customer's motivation. In this chapter we will look at the factors that influence consumer purchases, and examine how to construct promotions that address them.

Why People Buy

Buyer demand, in the perspective of traditional economics, has been viewed as a function of money, described as either income or wealth. But from the marketing point of view, money is not the only determinant of demand. It might not even be the major one.

The *ability to buy* is usually attributed to income and wealth; the *propensity to spend* is most likely determined by benefits offered customers. The *willingness to buy* results from individual motives, attitudes, expectations, needs, and wants.

Thus has arisen a multifaceted field of experts who approach buyer behavior from many disciplines, including psychology, sociology, anthropology and economics. They have discovered that whereas income and wealth are valid determinants of the *ability to buy,* the *propensity to spend* (or *willingness to buy)* depends on a variety of other factors.

A 1970s study by the Bureau of Labor Statistics revealed that blue-collar workers spent differently than did professionals and managers, even at the same level of income. The study showed an above-average percentage of money income spent among lower-income families for food, tobacco, personal care, and medical care. Higher-income families, on the other hand, spent a lesser proportion of income on automobiles, housing, eating out, alcoholic beverages, clothing, recreation, education, and travel.

The study also found that particular product purchases—like Scotch whiskey, pianos and organs, and expenditures connected with recreational boating—are not, as one might expect, confined to those with high income or wealth. These products are generally looked upon as symbolic of class status. Similarly, lower-income groups often purchased expensive, luxury brands.

Database-driven direct marketers have reported results like those of this study. Lifestyle variances need to be reckoned with, as do peer pressure and the influences of social class and other reference groups on the individual buyer. The study of differences in economic and demographic factors alone do not adequately explain variations in buying behavior. *Quantitative* analysis of markets is not enough. The direct marketer needs to know more about the *qualitative* aspects of buyer behavior in order to create benefits that motivate customers to purchase.

Intra-Personal Influences:
Physiological and Psychological Needs and Motivations

Any study of customer behavior, consumer *or* industrial, must begin with the *individual* and his or her physiological (biogenic) and psychological (psychogenic) needs.

It is *inherent* that a newborn baby cries when it is hungry. Later, though, it *learns* to cry to demonstrate that it is hungry. Direct marketing promotion techniques endeavor to affect the *learned* behavior of buyers. Learned needs evolve from the individual and the environment and are relatively slow to change.

A variety of so-called *learning theories* have been presented in the literature of psychology. Possibly one of the best known is "stimulus-response," demonstrated by Pavlov's experiments in which animal behavior patterns, influenced by rewards and punishments, ultimately became established habits. Seeing a perspiring athlete gulp down a soft drink in a television commercial, for example, might cause the observer to crave a similar refreshment.

Another area of learning experiences that has relevance for direct marketers is that of Gestalt or field theory. Such theory is concerned with the "whole" observation: the total scene including the observer's participation in it. As an example of Gestalt psychology, most of those looking at the configuration below will see tracks, trees, poles or six pairs of parallel lines; rarely will they see simply 12 vertical lines (try it!):

In terms of Gestalt theory, individuals tend to blend into their environment, of which they themselves are a part. Their lifestyles are frequently influenced by peer groups and they associate advertising messages with the credibility of the deliverer of such messages. Thus, a model in an advertisement wearing a hospital smock implies medical authority.

Psychoanalytic theories, including those of Sigmund Freud, postulate that *real buying motives may be hidden.* Motivation researchers, using the technique of the in-depth interview, have thrived providing their explanations of "hidden persuaders." Some such research has been controversial. In one motivation study done for the Forest Lawn Cemetery in California, it was determined that the bereaved "prefer large plots so that the deceased will have room to move about." That research also found a strong preference for caskets with locks since "many people fear that the dead will get out."

Abraham Maslow's Hierarchy of Needs developed a theory of motivation that ranked physical needs as basic, social needs next above, and actualization of self at the top of a pyramid. His ladder was labeled, bottom to top: physiological needs, safety needs, belongingness, esteem and self-actualization.

Inter-Personal Influences: The Impact of Environment on Behavior

Environmental influences—like class membership or that from family or other reference groups—also affect buyer behavior. In fact, some researchers see these factors as a more significant determinant of customer behavior than current income or accumulated wealth. Recent research suggests that these factors can even impact the behavior of industrial buyers.

Family and Household Reference Groups. Family and household groups of unrelated individuals living together frequently influence each other's buying decisions. Most often the decision is shared by spouses, but in a great many cases, children are the ultimate determinants. Some researchers have contended that the family or household are more proper units for observation than are individuals, because the decision-making process among family or household members is a significant variable in buying behavior.

Other Face-to-Face Small Reference Groups. "What our friends own we own, too . . . or shall soon own," said economist George Katona at the University of Michigan's Institute for Social Research. That is because face-to-face small reference groups—work associates, social acquaintances, religious affiliations, and, of course, neighbors—influence customer decisions.

"Keeping up with the Joneses" may explain the attributed direct marketing success of the prestigious *National Geographic* magazine when it mailed an invitation to subscribe to the next-door neighbors of its present subscribers. In substance, the direct-mail offer read: "Your next-door neighbor reads the *National Geographic*. Shouldn't you?"

More than one automobile manufacturer has experienced success, too, inviting neighbors to local dealers with a letter calling attention to a new model of their brand " . . . parked in your neighbor's driveway."

Referral selling, which uses a third party to directly or indirectly recommend a product or service, is a notable example of reference group influence which has special application for direct marketing. A customer is inclined to respect the judgments of friends or of an affinity group of which he or she is a member. That is why credit unions recommend products as diverse as insurance and automobiles to their members. That is also why oil companies sell socket wrench sets and luggage with inserts in their monthly bills going to their customers. And, referral recommendations from present customers have been shown to account for twenty percent or more of *new* customers acquired by direct marketing organizations soliciting customer referrals.

Social Class Influences. A buyer can be strongly influenced by his or her social class, or that to which he or she aspires. Noting that income level alone does not determine social class, researchers have pointed to type and location of housing, level of education, occupation, and *source* of income as being more important variables for defining social class membership. The beginning plumber and the just-out-of-school lawyer, for example, may have similar incomes but likely not the same social class memberships.

From a three-year study of the social structure of metropolitan Chicago, a research team headed by W. Lloyd Warner developed this social classification scheme:

Social Class	*Membership*
Upper-Upper	Old families and the traditional leaders
Lower-Upper	Socially prominent new rich
Upper-Middle	Professional and managerial successes
Lower-Middle	White-collar workers
Upper-Lower	Blue-collar workers
Lower-Lower	Unskilled workers and transients

Using this classification scheme, Warner and his colleagues determined that where and what a customer buys will differ not only by *economic* values but according to *symbolic* values. Studies such as this help explain the response power of an ego-building lead of a direct-mail letter like this one: "The list on which I found your name tells me that you are above-average in . . . etc."

Cultural Influences. Each of us is a product of our cultural heritage. We behave against the background of the culture from which we emerged, in which we grew up and in which we live. Unwittingly, we all respond—even as customers—to our cultural environment.

Many aspects of culture, such as courtship and status, are universal to all cultures. Some symbols, such as a young person's purchase of life insurance to signal independence, have telling influence on consumer behavior. The direct-response advertising copywriter needs to know which colors, phrases, or symbols are looked on favorably and which are taboo in a culture.

How Demand Affects an Offer

Just as consumer motivations influence response to an offer, so does marketplace demand. Price competition, so prevalent in the retail environment, matters less in direct marketing; more influential are other factors of *nonprice competition*, including product life cycle, product differentiation, positioning, brand preference, promotion, as well as market segmentation and customer behavior.

Nonprice competition is particularly prevalent in database-driven direct marketing because price comparison is not readily available to those who shop by mail or telephone. Price becomes subordinated to other benefits presented in a well-conceived promotion, including convenience, an attractive product presentation, and the seller's prestige, service and guarantees.

Price competition results in movements along a downward sloping demand curve, i.e., "the lower the price, the greater the demand." The objective of nonprice competition, however, is to shift the entire demand curve so as to reflect an increase in *total* demand at all levels of price, as shown in Figure 10.1.

Figure 10.1 visualizes how nonprice competition can increase total demand, through shifting the total demand curve to the right,

FIGURE 10.1

The nature of demand.

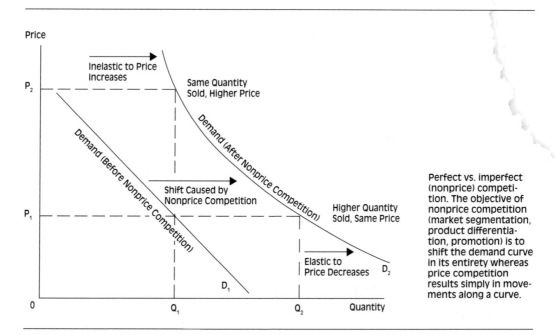

so that either a higher quantity of the product can be sold at the same price (P_1Q_2) or the same quantity can be sold at a higher price (P_2Q_1). Either is preferable to P_1Q_1!

A further objective of nonprice competition is to change the shape of the demand curve from a straight line (D_1) to a parabola (D_2), demonstrating that it becomes *inelastic* to price increases and *elastic* to price decreases. Thus, increases in price result in relatively small decreases in demand; decreases in price result in relatively large increases in demand.

Sometimes a price increase actually stimulates demand for a certain product. This is particularly true of products whose purchase is a way of impressing others—sometimes described as a "snob effect" or, as Thorstein Veblen called it, "conspicuous consumption." Likewise, sometimes a decrease in the price of particular goods leads to a decrease in demand. Such goods are termed *inferior*. In contrast, *superior* goods are those with higher prices that result in higher demand. Potatoes have been presented as an example of this phenomenon: the quantity purchased is thought to decline as price declines. A nineteenth-century economist, after whom the so-called Giffen Paradox is named, observed a substitution effect, of bread for potatoes, whenever the price of potatoes decreased.

Customers, through such substitutions, demonstrate their superior or inferior reputability in associating with goods that themselves are perceived to be superior or inferior.

The Offer and Its Benefits to Customers

Charles B. Mills, when asked why he was so adept at writing direct mail copy for O. M. Scott's grass seed, replied: "Because I like to talk about your lawn, not about my seed." Airlines sell a vacation in some exotic place, not the air trip to get there. Designers sell fashion and acceptance, not the practicality of clothing. Insurance companies sell security and peace of mind, not a paper contract. Elmer Wheeler, a longtime sales motivator, summed it up when he said, "Sell the sizzle, not the steak."

The manner of presentation of a promotion, coupled with the request for a response, encompasses what is commonly called an *offer*. The offer is concerned not only with the product and its pricing—including its differentiation for market segments—but also payment methods and terms, guarantees, and a host of other devices including no-obligation trials, sweepstakes, contests, gifts, premiums, time limits, and continuity clubs. Offers, incorporating customer benefits, are structured to incite action and overcome human inertia.

Next to the product and its benefit for a particular market segment, the offer is a key determinant of success or failure of a promotion strategy.

The paragraphs below are from a direct-mail offering of oil leases. Dated 1932, here is an example of the use of *persuasion:*

Dear Associate:

YOU MUST ACT THE VERY MINUTE YOU FINISH READING THIS LETTER—or else!—IF YOU FAIL,—IF YOU LET A SINGLE THING ON EARTH KEEP YOU OUT NOW————YOU MAY BE TURNING DOWN THE GREATEST CHANCE OF YOUR LIFE TO BECOME INDEPENDENTLY RICH—TO KNOW THE BLOOD SURGING THRILL OF THE BIGGEST!—

FATTEST!—FORTUNE IN CASH PROFITS YOU HAVE EVER HAD A CHANCE AT IN YOUR WHOLE LIFE!!

If you paid one bit of attention to my last two letters to you—you have instantly recognized that I am "ON THE TRAIL" of the very biggest thing we have ever had a chance at!!

Now you HAVE GOT TO ACT!!

YOU HAVE GOT TO ACT QUICK! BY RETURN MAIL—IF YOU ARE GOING TO GRASP THIS CHANCE TO PARTICIPATE IN ABSOLUTELY THE BIGGEST AND MOST ASTOUNDING—RECORD BREAKING,—PROFIT CLEAN UP WE HAVE EVER KNOWN!!

In my last letter I gave you an "inkling" of what I saw coming. I gave you a bare "thimble full" of the utterly amazing—brain staggering—mountainous mass of sensational advance information that has come to me!!

You know what I am telling you IS RIGHT—absolutely RIGHT! You KNOW the information I put in your hands in my last letter is CORRECT because the things I told you are IRREFUTABLE FACTS— FACTS . . . . I say!—that you can PUT YOUR FINGER ON— THAT YOU CAN EASILY . . . N-O-W . . . VERIFY!!—SITTING RIGHT IN YOUR OWN HOME!!

Now, contrast the preceding "get rich quick" persuasion with these paragraphs, also alluding to riches, from a truly classic *benefit-oriented* subscription offer sent by *Newsweek* magazine:

Dear Reader:

If the list upon which I found your name is any indication, this is not the first—nor will it be the last—subscription letter you receive. Quite frankly, your education and income set you apart from the general population and make you a highly rated prospect for everything from magazines to mutual funds.

You've undoubtedly "heard everything" by now in the way of promises and premiums. I won't try to top any of them.

Nor will I insult your intelligence.

If you subscribe to <u>Newsweek,</u> you won't get rich quick. You won't bowl over friends and business associates with clever remarks and sage comments after your first copy of <u>Newsweek</u>

arrives. (Your conversation will benefit from a better understanding of the events and forces of our era, but that's all. Wit and wisdom are gifts no magazine can bestow.) And should you attain further professional or business success during the term of your subscription, you'll have your own native ability and good luck to thank for it—not Newsweek.

What, then, can Newsweek do for you?

These examples aptly illustrate the evolution of direct-response advertising. Direct-marketing promotion experts now rely more on the selling value of *benefits* than on the hard sell of *persuasion*. Copy, design, and graphics are combined with arousing headlines and compelling *offers* in order to create an enticing impression, a favorable image.

The key sentence in the *Newsweek* letter may very well be the question: "What, then, can *Newsweek* do for you?" In fact, asking this question about any product or service is a great way to pinpoint benefits.

One technique for identifying benefits is called FAB analysis (*Features–Advantages–Benefits*). A well-publicized illustration of how FAB analysis works appears in Figure 10.2.

Direct Response Advertising: Message and Media

Direct response copywriting is an art. Those who have acquired the art and have achieved a track record of success are very much in demand. They have the ability to translate product features into advantages, these into benefits and benefits into words, design, and graphics.

Vic Schwab, who has such a track record, described long ago the copywriting art as "learning to think like a horse." As an illustration, he told the story of a farmer who had lost his horse. "How'd you find him so quickly?" asked a neighbor. To which the farmer replied: "Well, I just asked myself, if I were a horse, where would I go? I went there and there he was!"

Schwab used this story to drive home his copywriter's maxim that you have to "show people an advantage." This meant, to Schwab, that *you had to know them!* Today, databases provide that

FIGURE 10.2

Translating features into benefits.

Translating Features of a Washing Machine into Advantages and then into Benefits

Features (what the product has):
- compact size
- high spin speed
- wash temperature choice
- range of colors
- integrated tumble drier

Advantages (what the features do):
- fits into a smaller space
- clothes dry faster
- accommodates a full range of fabrics
- offers choice to consumer
- moves from wash to dry automatically

Benefits (why customers buy):
- space-saving
- time-saving
- does a good job
- flexibility
- convenience
- economy
- no more hand washing
- choices

How to get from features to benefits:
- . . . imagination
- . . . technology
- . . . product design
- . . . common sense

knowledge, enabling the trained copywriter to "think like a horse," to relate the benefits of the offer to customers.

Geared to a database, a personalized direct-mail letter can substitute for a personal call. The formats of direct mail are virtually unlimited, with many of them listed below:

Letter/Letterhead	Bulletins	Action Devices
Personalized	Price Lists	Order Forms
Lift Letters	Inserts	Applications
Memorandums	Reprints	Reply Envelopes
Cards	Audiotapes	Reply Cards
Self Mailers	Videotapes	Reply Labels
Circulars	Invitations	Mailing Envelopes
Folders	Survey Research	Package Inserts
Broadsides	Coupons	Billing Inserts
Brochures	Tickets	Cooperative
Booklets	Specialty Items	Mailings
Catalogs	Calendars	Syndicated
Publications	Novelties	Mailings

Of all these various formats of direct mail, however, the basic format is this one:

- Mailing Envelope

- Letter (preferably, database-personalized)

- Circular (only if needed)

- Order Form

- Return Envelope

How long should a direct-mail letter be? Abraham Lincoln, when asked how long a man's legs should be, wisely replied that they should be just long enough to touch the ground. Similarly, a letter should be long enough to say what it has to say. No longer. No shorter. As for the admonition "no one reads long copy," that is best taken with a grain of salt!

Some prefer to write letters by formula in order to keep the copy flowing in a logical manner. There are many to choose from. One is labeled "*A–I–D–A*," initial letters of:

- Attract *Attention*
- Arouse *Interest*
- Stimulate *Desire*
- Call for *Action*

Another formula is labeled *"P–P–P–P,"* initial letters of:

- *Picture*—get attention early in the copy
- *Promise*—describe the product's benefits to the reader
- *Prove*—show value of the product or service
- *Push*—ask for the order

Bob Stone's Seven-Step Formula has also stood the test of time:

1. Promise a benefit in your headline or first paragraph.
2. Immediately enlarge on your most important benefit.
3. Tell the reader specifically what he or she will get.
4. Back up your statements with proofs and endorsements.
5. Tell the reader what will be lost by not acting.
6. Rephrase your prominent benefits in the closing offer.
7. Incite action now.

The promotion formats of direct-response advertising other than direct mail can be basically categorized as:

- Print media—magazines and newspapers
- Broadcast media—television and radio
- Interactive electronic media—telephone, television, and personal computers

Direct-response advertising in newspapers and magazines can be effective but message space is limited compared to direct-mail packages or catalogs. Like catalog copy, the headline must gain attention quickly and the body copy must tell the story completely yet concisely. The copy, as always, must be benefit-oriented and the graphic design should lead the reader through the advertisement's elements in the sequence intended. Illustrations augment copy. A response device must be provided, of course.

Television's limitations for direct-response advertisers have been its high cost and the short duration of an individual commercial message. The advent of cable television, including emerging interactive features, has made possible more *directed* messages and even market segmentation. This has increased the effectiveness (results vs. costs) of the television medium.

Radio has had practical limitations, too. Most radio listeners are driving an automobile or are otherwise occupied, and telephones or pencil and pad are out of reach. Because radio does not provide the opportunity to visualize, it is most effective with known products or those which do not require demonstration. Radio, as well as television, have both been successfully used as a *support* medium, calling attention to forthcoming print or direct-mail messages.

Interactive electronic media—notably, the telephone—are an integral part of direct marketing. These media, like direct mail but unlike print or broadcast, offer two-way communication: they can be utilized for response (inbound) as well as for advertising (outbound). Telephones, allied through a modem with personal computers, now provide visualization and demonstration along with a printed record. A similar alliance is occurring with FAX machines. Soon, black boxes will extend interactivity, wired and wireless with TV sets.

An integral part of this interactivity has been and continues to be the salesperson. Personal selling—including selling by telephone—can provide person-to-person, two-way communication, because a salesperson can listen and use feedback to tailor promotional messages to individual buyers. While a personal sales call can be tremendously expensive, if a prospective customer is qualified, serious, and sincerely interested, a personal sales call can be worthwhile.

Direct marketing can incorporate elements of the personal sales call. The sales presentation may be contained in printed or broadcast direct-response advertising messages, or a mail-order package. A salesperson might speak to customers by telephone, or call on a qualified prospect who has been identified through a lead-generating program. Similarly, a catalog from a retail store might cause the recipient to visit the store, where a salesperson can complete the transaction.

CASE STUDY

Utilizing the Promotional Mix in Direct Marketing

This case demonstrates how direct marketing used all four forms of promotion—advertising, selling, publicity, and sales promotion—to support Missouri Repertory Theater (MRT).

MRT was founded in 1964 by Dr. Patricia McIlrath, who early on believed that direct marketing could achieve a mix of earned and contributed revenue that would help accomplish her vision of artistic success. An initial hat-in-hand budget of $3,500 for direct-mail advertising to sell season tickets grew a hundredfold as the years went by. While other nonprofit organizations sought a mix of one-third earned income and two-thirds contributions, MRT's objective was *two-thirds* earned.

Building a database of season subscribers and individuals provided a number of opportunities. MRT could draw on the database for continuity selling of season tickets to single ticket buyers, and cross selling of tickets to other events. It also provided buyer profiles that guided new-customer acquisition efforts. ZIP code areas became a major qualifier for targeting direct mail to prospects.

Single-ticket buyers, who could not be economically reached through the medium of direct mail, were garnered from response advertisements in demographically selected print and broadcast media. Individual performance buyers were identified and upgraded to season tickets, with an average of four single-ticket purchases occurring before that transition happened.

Advertising media expanded from direct mail to newspapers, which solicited a direct response by mail or by telephone. Thirty-second spots were used on television with longer spots on radio. Outdoor billboards promoting seasonal performances of Charles Dickens' *Christmas Carol* featured an easy-to-remember local telephone number: "Dial 'DIC-KENS' for your reserved tickets." *Christmas Carol* and other special events became database-driven cross-selling promotion opportunities.

Personal sales calls also helped build support. Businesses and other organizations were called on personally by staff *salespeople* who rendered personal assistance in making tickets readily available to members or employees of these organizations. Direct mail was used extensively to initially contact groups and businesses, both to solicit direct orders as well as to generate inquiries for personal sales follow-up.

Personal sales calls also played a role in soliciting contributions from public and private foundations as well as individual and business donors.

Telemarketing has been an important medium for closing sales and box-office personnel have been trained in the nuances of personal selling.

Before and during its season, MRT publicizes its programs extensively in metropolitan, suburban, and rural publications, television and radio in six states. Such publicity includes stories about the productions, human interest features, interviews with the cast and directors, as well as critical reviews of performances.

Sales support promotion included a slide presentation for showing to organizations and groups. Support also included posters, bumper stickers, two-for-one coupons for special performances, tie-ins with area restaurants, discounts to senior citizens as well as students and incentives to convert single-ticket buyers to season subscribers.

During 30 years of planned growth, MRT's Dr. McIlrath consistently credited an orientation to direct marketing with achieving nearly 70 percent of its operating budget from earned revenue. This achievement, coupled with near-capacity audiences, is considered highly significant among cultural and arts groups.

11

Success Stories in Keeping and Cultivating Customers

Successful customer relationships put the customer in the driver's seat. They occur when market-driven organizations provide everything their customers want: quality, value, and service.

These organizations cultivate relationships by maintaining contact before, during, and after the sale. They are there when their customer needs them. They quickly correct errors. They *remember* how it feels to be a customer.

They use their customer databases to stay *close* to the customer. They listen, too, using 800-number telephone lines and monitoring comment cards, unsolicited mail, and focus groups for clues on how they are doing. And they work hard to deliver on their promises and make good on complaints.

It's no wonder that these companies are able to create lasting customer relationships that profit both the customer and the company. Let's look at a few who have succeeded.

Some Ways to Benefit from the Continuity of Customer Relationships

When Sears sells an appliance, it makes a dozen "promises" about its service and delivery—and then bends over backwards to live up to them.

When a customer complains about a battery that is "dead" when purchased, Duracell will quickly replace it, sending along a coupon for obtaining additional batteries without cost and a postage-paid label for returning the defunct battery.

Both of these efforts toward customer continuity stand in contrast to United Way, which seems to limit continuity efforts to its customers' working lives. When a regular contributor retires or otherwise severs his or her relationship with the company that solicited donations, United Way does not attempt to solicit additional money because it is "too cumbersome" to include the ultimate customer, the contributor, in its database!

More and more organizations, especially retailers, are adopting customer retention strategies like those used by Sears and Duracell. Many of these strategies use interactive technology to establish affinity and continuity of relationships. Loyalty programs, such as those directed to frequent flyers or frequent buyers, would be impossible without a customer database.

Embassy Suites wrote a guest within days after a stay:

Dear Valued Guest:

As a result of our busy day-to-day schedules, it is often difficult for us to meet each other and to speak personally about your experience at our hotel.

I often hear from our guests who have had positive experiences, and of course, I sometimes hear from those guests who have unexpected problems. But most of our guests come and go without any immediate responses to their stay at Embassy Suites. To know if our guests were truly satisfied with their stay, we must wait and see if they return for another visit.

Obviously, we won't stay in business for very long with one-time customers . . .

Amoco Oil Company thanks customers ". . . for maintaining your outstanding credit rating." Sometimes, it's a line or two on a statement; other times, a "thank you" letter includes a cross-selling invitation ". . . to take advantage of a special offer."

The Salvation Army promotes continuity this way:

Dear Donor:

The "Heat for Life/Project Warmth" has passed as has winter, but we want to let you know how grateful we are for your gift.

You helped some 60 community agencies warm the hearts and houses of thousands over this past winter.

And your gift is continuing to work as we serve the needs of your community.

Thank you.

(. . . followed by a return form offering to tell the donor about a variety of other Salvation Army services . . .)

And, airlines have their own "secret weapon" for continuity:

CONGRATULATIONS! YOU'VE QUALIFIED
FOR YOUR <u>NEW</u> FREQUENT FLIGHT BONUS CARD!

Dear Frequent Flight Bonus Cardholder:

I'm pleased to enclose your <u>new</u> Frequent Flight Bonus Card. Beginning right now, it replaces your old card—and it entitles you to <u>continue</u> enjoying Frequent Flight Bonus Card offers for another full year, with our compliments . . . and thanks.

<u>Enjoy "preferred traveler" service whenever you fly.</u>

Virtually every airline, hotel, and car rental has its customer re-ward program for travel continuity. Many of these have become affinity groups, extending their influence to "travel partners" such as cruise lines, and even to non-travel services such as credit cards. One major hotel has offered ". . . a limited number of prominent local citizens the opportunity to join (its) prestigious 'For Members Only' club (to) receive privileges, benefits and values . . . not available to the general public."

Buick, historically frequent purchaser of mass-market print and broadcast media, including the Super Bowl game, turned to direct marketing to amass a list of targets for its 1992 Roadmaster. Long-time Buick customers received an opportunity to request a PC disk that detailed the car along with every other 1992 Buick model.

Once installed, the disk gave the Buick customer a graphic demonstration of the new 8-cylinder engine as well as the rear-wheel drive features of this car. The workings and safety benefits of the airbag and anti-lock braking systems were also demonstrated through animation. The loyal customer then was able to price every model and every option as well as to pick colors.

As a result, when one 30-year customer went to his long-time dealer to purchase, he was already pre-sold. The dealer, recalling the customer's obsession with black Buicks in prior purchases, greeted him with: "I knew that if I put that shiny, new black Buick Roadmaster in the window, you'd come in and buy it."

The dealer was wrong. Buick's benefit-laden direct response advertising had lured the customer to the dealer. Once there, the dealer closed the sale, delivered and serviced the car in a manner that retained an already-excellent customer relationship.

The dealer also saw to it that this customer was updated in the Buick database—because he was a Buick *CUSTOMER!* Regular mail and telephone communications remind him of that. Information thus perpetuates his relationship and keeps him loyal to Buick.

Well-timed direct mail arrives when it is appropriate for an upgrade to a later model. A post-purchase telemarketing effort comes shortly after delivery of the new car, followed by a mailed satisfaction survey. Cross selling offers an extension of the standard car warranty period, a maintenance service package, regular service reminders—even personal accident insurance and a catalog of unrelated "Buick Motorsports Apparel!"

Buick's "image" advertising on television and in other media—much of it benefit-oriented and response-driven—reinforces the customer's relationship at the same time as it seeks to acquire more new customers just like him. By coupling ongoing image advertising with tests of new database refinements, market segments, and benefit-oriented promotion offers, Buick's ongoing *customer relationship* marketing is sure to keep all the new customers it acquires!

Some Ways to Maximize Cross-Selling Opportunities

During a recession, retailers and manufacturers seem to concentrate on *cultivating* customers rather than *creating* customers. They focus on getting current customers to spend more, instead of spending more to lure new customers. So Saks Fifth Avenue has used catalogs to create store traffic as well as mail and telephone orders. And the director of database marketing for a major packaged goods company allocated 95 percent of his unit's budget to selling more of its well-known brands to present customers.

Opportunities for cross selling and upgrading are abundant.

Southwestern Bell Telephone Company has offered out-of-the-ordinary listings in its telephone directories for $3 a month, with this insert in its monthly billing:

Increase the value of your listing

Your listing in the phone book's residence section can stand out like never before. Now, with a Signature Listing™, you can have your name and residential phone number in script or bold similar to the bold listings once reserved for business customers. And you can choose from two Signature Listings:

Contemporary Bold:	Sophisticated Script:
John Doe	*John Doe*
Mary Doe	*Mary Doe*

Immediately after purchasing a new Buick, a customer received this letter from National General Insurance Company, a General Motors Insurance Company:

AN IMPORTANT NEW BENEFIT LINKED TO OWNERSHIP
OF THE FOLLOWING GENERAL MOTORS VEHICLE
Please mail the enclosed REQUEST within 14 days for fastest service

1992 Buick Roadmaster ltt Limited   Vehicle ID#: 1G4BT-5373NR4-27595

As the owner of a Buick Roadmaster ltt Limited, you have an opportunity to take advantage of a special offer.

Effective immediately, you have the right to request a Free Quote on a GM benefit that could save you $50, $100, $150 a year on vehicle insurance. This is important so please read carefully.

Hewlett-Packard, reacting to a warranty registration for a new calculator, mailed the customer an offer of a "Support Agreement" for it. Presumably reacting to the same database, Grapevine Publications, Inc. sent a mail-order offer of a training guide for the product. Microsoft Windows customers have been sent cross-selling offers of Microsoft Word for Windows and Microsoft Excel. WordPerfect users have been cross-sold utility software and business stationery.

Time Life Multi Mail, a subsidiary of Time Warner, Inc., distributes direct mail packages with offers from a variety of advertisers. Importantly, these packages are targeted to customers, categorized by special interests, who have bought something from Time Life within the previous two years. Categories have included cooking and crafts; health and fitness; products aimed at Time Life Gold customers.

This letter, inserted in a Lands' End mail-order brochure, provided an exclusive cross-sell offer from the Walt Disney World Resort in Florida:

Dear Lands' End Customer:

We've recently begun talking with Walt Disney World about partnering on some projects, both here in the USA and abroad. A relationship seemed a natural, in part because we share the same feelings about exceeding your expectations in everything we do.

Recently, we visited the Walt Disney World Resort in Florida and got a look at the soon-to-be-opened Wilderness Lodge. It's pretty amazing. We said we'd tell you and other Lands' End customers about it in this brochure. And the Disney people reciprocated by putting together some customized vacation packages exclusively for our hardworking Lands' End employees and valued customers like you.

In the meantime, thanks for shopping with Lands' End!

An Example of Cross-Selling from Mail Order

Households and businesses provided with personalized checks through their financial institutions typically are supplied these by a unit of Deluxe Check Printers. Cross-selling begins with delivery of the printed checks.

An insert with the order offers upgrades to monogrammed or otherwise distinctive personalized checks on reorder. Another insert cross-sells an assortment of personalized pre-inked rubber stamps for imprinting return addresses, deposit endorsements, notices such as "Past Due," or simple fun logos.

Those "Preferred Customers" ordering such items soon hear from a division of Deluxe Check Printers, Delmart's Top Drawer Home Office Products. Offers from this division include desk reference calendars, brief cases, calculators, personal security safes, desk lamps and clocks, note pads, phones and answering machines, and a variety of other office products.

Cross-selling then extends beyond office products to special occasion gifts for Mother's Day, Father's Day, graduation and weddings: vintage radios, personalized stationery, decorator wall clocks and travel clocks, pen & pencil sets, and golf balls.

In a self-identifying situation such as this, the opportunities for cross-selling to customers captured in a database are endless!

WORKSHOP

Old American Insurance Company's "Building-a-Customer" Program

In 1939, when Thomas McGee & Sons began to offer personal insurance to older Americans who were largely bypassed by traditional insurance agents, senior citizens were a widely dispersed, difficult to reach minority group. The best strategy for reaching them seemed to be mail order—a completely new strategy for selling insurance.

At that time, no one had compiled a list of senior citizens —no one, that is, except the Departments of Motor Vehicles of the various states issuing driver's licenses. These early public records contained a wealth of customer-identifying factors, including color of eyes and hair, weight, and date of birth.

Now, here was more than a list. Here was a *database*. It was now up to McGee & Sons (through its newly-formed "Old American Insurance Company") to compile this senior citizen market segment from driver's license records. And they did.

Let's look at the process of customer creation, followed by continuity selling and cross-selling, as Old American Insurance pioneered it in its *Building-a-Customer* program.

Initially, Old American engaged in direct sales through mail order, without involving an agent. Later, it applied its expertise in direct marketing to lead-generation programs for agency sales.

Old American's Direct Sales Model of Building Relationships

An older-age prospect, identified from a database mailing list, might first become a policyholder of Old American Insurance Company through purchase of an introductory term of its Senior Accident Policy, from a solicitation like this . . .

You are invited to spend 25¢ and receive 30 days of coverage under Old American Insurance Company's $25,000 Senior Accident Policy . . .

Upon conversion from the 30 days' introductory term, or following a subsequent renewal, the policyholder might be sent a "thank you" letter like this one, along with an application form to pass along to "another member of the family:"

Dear Policyholder:

Thank you for renewing your Senior Accident Policy. Your payment has been received and we have extended your coverage for the full period you requested.

You made the right decision to continue your Senior Accident protection. Now you can face the future more confidently, knowing that in case you have a covered accident, you'll be able to claim important cash benefits right when you need the money most.

Since you're a satisfied policyholder, I'm asking you to share this protection with others. That's why I've enclosed a Senior Accident Policy application for you to give to another member of your family. You'll see it makes the same offer that you took advantage of.

There is also enclosed with this letter a reply card on which can be listed names and addresses of friends and other relatives to whom you would like us to mail information on the insurance policies we offer . . .

Later comes one of a variety of offers to *increase* the value of the coverage *initially* provided by the Senior Accident Policy.

The Senior Accident policyholder may also need supplemental life insurance. So, a cross-selling offer follows, inviting the customer to buy *another product*—Guaranteed Acceptance Life Insurance—with the offer stating ". . . the plain facts about our revolutionary plan of life insurance that guarantees to accept you if you are between the ages of 50 and 80."

To express appreciation and strive for continuity, the customer might be sent, a month or so in advance of the life insurance policy's renewal date, a reproduction of a Norman Rockwell illustration suitable for framing.

From its increasingly sophisticated database, Old American now observes that its customer is approaching the age of eligibility for

Medicare and quite likely will need private coverage to *supplement* Medicare benefits in order to reimburse the deductible and co-pay amounts.

So, Old American writes its customer again:

HOW CAN YOU SAY "NO"
TO OUR INVITATION
TO TAKE A FREE LOOK AT
OUR MEDICARE-PLUS POLICY?

Dear Customer:

You can't possibly say "no"—it would be imprudent to pass up this offer to apply for this Medicare supplemental plan . . . for people 65 and over . . . for a full 30 days.

I believe you can only say "yes" once you see all the benefits this plan provides. And you do not have to send any money to apply.

Still another product—a Cancer Indemnity Protection Policy — might be offered to specific customers about whom Old American has information in its comprehensive database. The offer reads:

Here's some of the best news you'll
ever hear about coping with cancer!

Get this book free —
CANCER . . . There's Hope —

Just for reviewing our
CANCER INDEMNITY
PROTECTION POLICY . . .

The gift book by H&R Block co-founder, Richard Bloch, tells how he used his positive mental attitude, prayer, and the will to fight, to beat his malignancy, which had been diagnosed as terminal.

Here's a last example—but certainly not *all* that Old American did—to *create, care for, keep, and cultivate customers* . . . whose lifetime value turned out to be its greatest asset.

The company wanted its customers to examine and be protected temporarily by a new product: coverage for surgical procedures. It sent each customer an actual personalized policy labeled—

OFFICIAL POLICYHOLDER NOTIFICATION
Valuable Insurance Policy
Enclosed for Old American Policyholder:

(The Customer's Name/Address)

In force, right now
at no cost to you!

The envelope containing this document was stamped "Handle With Care" . . . which applied to the policy *and* the customer!

Old American's Agency Sales Model of Building Relationships

Twenty-five years into its success story with the mail-order sale of personal insurance to senior citizens, Old American discovered through research and experimenting that a *salesperson* could be more effective than a letter at the point-of-sale.

Drawing on its mail-order experience, expertise, and resources, the company developed a database-driven direct marketing system called Planned Production. The market definition of the database was the same for both the direct and agency distribution systems. So were the products . . . and the promotion. An agent, however, would concentrate in a geographic area defined by ZIP codes and actually achieve the same or greater sales results as one working a much larger, though not defined, area.

The nucleus of the Planned Production system was described as *Territorial Direct Mail*. Various mailing programs, developed and fulfilled by the company, featured specific products. Cost was shared by the company and agent to assure proper follow-up. Inquiries came back to the company for recording and analysis, before being forwarded to the agent for action.

The second element of Planned Production—described as *Company Referrals*—was derived from Old American's mail-order policyholder database, the records of active and inactive *direct sales* customers. The agent was given the option of calling on these customers for servicing, reinstating lapsed coverages, or offering additional coverages. Also provided were data for the agent's own policyholders in the area, "orphan" policyholders (those without an agent active) as well as the beneficiaries and referrals of current customers.

Agent Referrals, also captured in a database, were a third element of the system. Typically, these resulted from a call on a lead or a company referral. In the course of the follow-up, the prospect often recommended someone—a neighbor, a work associate, a friend, a relative—whom the prospect felt might have an interest in the product presented by the agent.

A fourth element of Planned Production was called "FUN," an acronym for *follow-up* of *non*-respondents. These were the names of those in the prospect database who had received the direct mail promotion but had *not* responded. Agents who called on these non-respondents made an interesting discovery: 25 percent of them granted interviews! From that point in the selling process, the closure rate was the same as that from leads.

The final element of the Planned Production agency sales system, as with direct sales, was that of *Building-a-Customer*. Through inserts with premium billing as well as solo direct mail, active customers were offered increases to their existing coverages. They were also provided the opportunity to request information about other Old American Insurance Company products.

V

Customers: Why to Cultivate Them

Customers are the lifeblood of your business . . . and one of its major assets. In Part V, we will examine how to place a value on your customer list, and determine exactly how much to invest in acquiring new customers.

12

Customers Are Your Most Valuable Asset

The value of customers is more than that shown on a line, sometimes found on balance sheets, called "goodwill." Customers have *intrinsic* value, because the first sale to a newly acquired customer is but a forerunner of additional sales to that customer in the future. And since they are a source of future revenues and future profits, customers need to be viewed as intangible *assets* of an organization, just as are tangible buildings, equipment, inventory, and accounts receivable.

However, relatively few organizations "capitalize" their costs of acquiring customers as they do these other assets—even though customers constitute their most valuable asset.

Because direct marketers are concerned with ongoing relationships and affinity through continuity selling and cross selling, they view the *lifetime value of a customer* (LTV) as an asset—variously called *deferred acquisition cost* or *prepaid advertising*—even though it doesn't show up on the balance sheet!

LTV, too, is the direct marketer's determinant for promotion budgeting. While most firms traditionally use the percent-of-sales method for budgeting advertising, viewing it as an expense, direct marketers consider advertising as an investment, relating objective sales revenues to the need for and the cost of acquiring and retaining customers. (A fallacy of the traditional method, of course, is that advertising is viewed as a *result,* rather than a *cause,* of sales.)

Direct marketers know that if a direct marketing action results in the acquisition of *new* customers who will generate value over time and in the long run, then that action may be desirable even though the initial "response per thousand" does not recapture the initial expenditure. This chapter shows how direct marketers decide what a customer is worth—and how much can be spent to acquire a new one.

"What Should My Response Rate Be?"

There is no universal answer to this question, possibly the most frequently asked question in direct marketing. There is no universally "normal" expectation. Response varies depending on the product and its demand, price competition, market preference, and the nature of the promotional offer. Furthermore, response will vary widely according to the pre-qualification of the database used. Typically, all other factors being equal, *present customers* will respond to an offer for a new product at a much higher level than will non-qualified *cold prospects*.

More realistically, the question should be rephrased to ask: "What response do I *need*?" Or, even more apropos, *"What is the value of a customer?"* Or, what lesser level of response would be required in order to *break even* over an extended period of time during which a new customer demonstrates value through repurchases or additional purchases?

Determination of Break-Even

Profit maximization occurs at the point at which marginal revenue equals marginal cost. That is, the revenue derived from the sale of one *additional* unit is equal to the cost of producing that unit. When the cost of producing each additional unit rises, the average cost of all units produced also rises, so that average profit, the residual between average revenue and average cost, decreases.

Total *production* costs are generally a combination of *fixed* and *variable* costs. Fixed costs, such as plant and equipment depreciation and maintenance, remain fairly constant regardless of the volume of production (up to a point!); variable costs, such as raw materials, generally increase proportionate to the level of production.

Direct marketers must also be concerned with *promotion* costs, the costs of acquiring customers. Promotion costs also have fixed and variable elements. Relatively fixed, for example, are costs of creating a direct-mail package, a print or broadcast direct-response advertisement. Other costs, such as printing, paper, and postage, typically increase in proportion to volume.

But promotion costs associated with direct marketing, once the expenditure has occurred, might all be considered fixed costs. Such an expenditure, once made, is the same, whether one or 1,000 orders result. In contrast, a salesperson's commission is a variable cost, paid only if a sale is consummated.

Figure 12.1 presents two points—one that includes only production costs and one with both production and promotion costs included. *Production* break-even (B/E) *without direct marketing promotion costs* occurs at point A, when total revenue (TR) is equal to total *production* costs (TPC). Total production costs, in turn, consist of the combination of fixed production costs (FPC) and variable production costs (VPC). VPC, as shown, usually increases less rapidly as production volume increases, ultimately reaching an optimum level of increase. These costs begin to accelerate once more as plant capacity is exceeded.

To the left of the TR line and under the TPC line is an area in which there is a total production loss (TPL) as the economies of scale have not yet been reached. Beyond that point, TR divided by the quantity sold minus TPC divided by the quantity sold is equal to a *unit profit (UP)*, which is break-even, at point A, *without promotion costs*, thus:

$$TR/Q - TPC/Q = UP$$

Unit profit is, in effect, the limit of the promotion budget absent any continuity or cross selling to the newly acquired customer. While traditional break-even calculation includes promotion as an overhead expense, along with production costs, the direct marketer views promotion costs—the costs of advertising and selling; customer acquisition and retention—differently.

For illustration, assume that a direct-response promotion consists of an offer mailed to 250M prospects at a cost of $500/M pieces mailed, a total promotion cost (TPRC) of $125,000. Super-imposing this $125,000 promotion cost (TPRC) on TPC, which varies with total production volume, it is apparent that sales must be

FIGURE 12.1
Break-even determination.

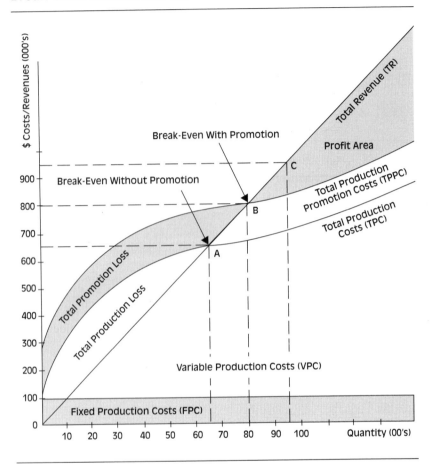

increased by 1,500 units, from the production break-even of 6,500 units to the production *plus promotion* break-even of 8,000 units.

In this illustration, therefore, average promotion costs per thousand pieces mailed (APRC/M) divided by UP becomes break-even at point B *with promotion,* thus:

$$APRC/M \div UP = B/E$$

Note that total sales in units per thousand pieces mailed (TS/M) less break-even sales per thousand pieces mailed (B/E Sales/M) multiplied by the UP becomes equal to net profit per thousand pieces mailed, at point C, thus:

$$\text{TS/M} - \text{B/E SALES/M} \times \text{UP} = \text{NET PROFIT/M}$$

To break-even, the cost of making a sale and acquiring a customer cannot exceed unit profit for that sale. Let's look next at an example where there is only one sale, no continuity.

Establishing the Break-Even Point for a Single Sale

Establishing the break-even point for a single sale to a new customer is a first step. Here's the formula:

$$\frac{\textit{Promotion Cost}}{\textit{Unit Profit per Sale}} = \textit{Break-Even Number of Sales}$$

That is, if the direct marketer recovers promotion cost from the gross profit (beyond cost-of-goods-sold and overhead) of the total number of units sold, he or she breaks even *on those sales*.

Figure 12.2 provides a profit worksheet useful for calculating the break-even point and profit at various levels of unit sales per thousand pieces of mail promotion. A variation of this can be used for print or broadcast promotion.

Lines 2 through 8 represent production costs, totaling $17.69 (line 9) per copy of *Practical Mathematics*. Order processing/collection costs (line 5) and costs of returns (line 6) are amortized and allocated to net sales. These calculations are also shown in Figure 12.2 as are certain assumptions.

Unit profit (line 10) is calculated by subtracting $17.69 from the book's selling price of $39.95 (line 1). This gross profit, when divided into total promotion costs of $345.83 per M pieces mailed (line 11), provides break-even net sales per thousand pieces mailed (line 12), which is 15.54 or 1.55 percent—the answer to the question: *"What response do I need?"*

Having calculated a break-even response rate of 1.55 percent, lines 13 through 20 of Figure 12.2 present alternative profit amounts at assumed alternative levels of net sales.

FIGURE 12.2
Direct marketing profit worksheet.

Product/Offer: *Practical Mathematics* @ $39.95, net 30 days

Assumptions:		Order Processing/Collection Costs:		Cost of Returns:	
# Promotions Mailed	9,508	Gross Orders	100 @ $1.80 = $180.00	Return Servicing	$1.30
Shipments Returned	8%	Less: Returns	8 @ 8% of 100	Shipping/Delivery	$2.20
Sales Uncollectable	6%	Net Sales	(A) 92 @ $0.50 = $46.00	Total (C)	$3.50
		Total	(B) $226.00	Returns Projected (D)	8%
		Cost Per Net Sale (B/A) =	$2.46	Cost Per Net Sale (C × D/1.00 − D)	$0.30

Break-Even Calculation:

Line	Description			
1	Selling Price		$39.95	
2	Cost-of-Goods Sold	$5.99		
3	G & A Allocation	$3.80		
4	Shipping/Delivery Costs	$2.20		
5	Processing/Collection Costs	$2.46		
6	Cost of Returns	$0.30		
7	Sales Uncollectable	$2.40		
8	Premium Gift Cost	$0.54		
9	Total Production Costs		$17.69	
10	Unit Profit (Line 1 − Line 9)		$22.26	
11	Total Promotion Costs per M Pieces Mailed (includes database, print, mail, postage, overhead)		$345.83	
12	Breakeven Net Sales/M Pieces Mailed (Line 11/Line 12)		15.54	

Total Profit at Alternative Levels of Net Sales:

13	Projected Net Sales per M Pieces Mailed	17	20	25	30	35	40	45
14	Less: Break-even Sales (Line 12)	15.54	15.54	15.54	15.54	15.54	15.54	15.54
15	Net Sales Earning Full Unit Profit (Line 13 − Line 14)	1.46	4.46	9.46	14.46	19.46	24.46	29.46
16	Unit Profit (Line 10)	$22.26	$22.26	$22.26	$22.26	$22.26	$22.26	$22.26
17	Net Profit per M Pieces Mailed (Line 15 × Line 16)	$32.61	$99.39	$210.69	$322.00	$433.30	$544.61	$655.91
18	M Pieces Mailed	9,508	9,508	9,508	9,508	9,508	9,508	9,508
19	Total Net Profit (Line 17 × Line 18/1000)	$310.01	$944.98	$2,003.26	$3,061.55	$4,119.83	$5,178.11	$6,236.40
20	Net Profit as % of Net Sales: Line19/(Line1 × Line13 × Line18/1000)	4.80%	12.44%	21.10%	26.87%	30.99%	34.08%	36.49%

PAR: The Continuity Value of a Customer Over Time

Relatively few direct marketers enjoy the luxury of breaking even on the *first* sale from a *new* customer, as just illustrated. Rather, there is more likely to be an *investment* in that customer, which will be returned through *future* sales.

PAR is *the continuity value of a customer over future time.* Like the lifetime value of a customer (LTV), PAR is an objective.

PAR can be calculated in this way:

1. Develop a stream of *total revenues* over a period of future time, taking into account an assumed frequency of reorder or renewal as well as an assumed dollar revenue of reorder or renewal. Provide, too, for *attrition*, the assumed (historic) lapse or expire rate from one future time period to the next.

2. From this total revenue stream, deduct for each time period the cost-of-goods-sold as well as general administrative expenses. The residuals thus derived represent a series of contributions for defraying promotion costs associated with acquiring new customers—together with, ultimately, producing a profit.

3. This stream of contributions, then, is discounted to a *present value* at some rate appropriate to the risk of investing in new customers.

In insurance selling, PAR measures the ongoing value of the *initial* sale of a *single* insurance policy as it is *renewed, increased, kept in force.* It can also measure the value of magazine subscription renewals, record or book club sales or future catalog purchases—all instances of *continuity selling.*

An example of calculating the continuity value of a customer is shown in Figure 12.3. Projected over a 5-year period, an initial base of 100 customers is assumed, as is a retention rate of 65 percent at the beginning of the second year; 80 percent of those remaining at the beginning of the third year; 85 percent entering the fourth year; 90 percent entering the fifth year. Gross sales revenue is assumed to increase 5 percent annually.

Costs-of-goods-sold plus general administrative costs and a target profit of 10 percent on sales, which is optional as an assumption, are estimated as percentages of revenues. These rates are as-

FIGURE 12.3
PAR, the continuity value of a customer over time

ASSUME:

(1) Retention Rates

Year 1 = 100.00%   of New Customers
Year 2 = 65.00%   of Year 1
Year 3 = 80.00%   of Year 2
Year 4 = 85.00%   of Year 3
Year 5 = 90.00%   of Year 4

(2) Gross $ Revenue:

	# Active Customers		Annual Revenues /Customer		Gross Annual Revenues
Year I:	100	×	$50	=	$5,000
Year 2:	65	×	$53	=	$3,445
Year 3:	52	×	$55	=	$2,860
Year 4:	44	×	$58	=	$2,564
Year 5:	40	×	$60	=	$2,387

(3) Fulfillment Costs:

Costs of Goods Sold = 40.00% (includes handling, recording, reporting, communications, etc.)
Gen./Admin.Costs = 20.00% (includes all administrative costs and overhead.)
Target % on Sales = 10.00%
Total Costs = 70.00%

(4) Gross Profit = Contribution to Acquisition Cost . . . (2) – (3).

(5) Present Value of Future Sales . . . Discount of Future Gross Profits.

(6) Present Value of a Customer . . . i.e., the amount of money which can be spent to acquire a new customer.

PROJECT:

	# Active Customers (1) @	Gross Annual Revenues (2)	Total Costs ×	(3) = Amount	Gross Profits (4)	×	10% Discount Factor %	Present Customers = (5)
Year 1:	100	$5,000	70.00%	$3,500	$1,500	×	1.0000	$1,500.00
Year 2:	65	$3,445	70.00%	$2,412	$1,034	×	0.9091	$939.55
Year 3:	52	$2,860	70.00%	$2,002	$858	×	0.8264	$709.05
Year 4:	44	$2,564	70.00%	$1,795	$769	×	0.7513	$577.81
Year 5:	40	$2,387	70.00%	$1,671	$716	×	0.6831	$489.13

Discounted Present Value of 100 Customers: $4,215.54

Present Value of a Customer (divide by 100): $42.16 (6)

Break-even thus would require, at a cost/M pieces mailed of $421.60, a response rate of 1% in order to recover costs over a five-year projection of customer activity.

sumed to be constant over the five-year projection, although in reality this is seldom the case.

With these assumptions, together with an assumed 10 percent discount factor, the present value of a customer is calculated to be $42.16. This, then, is the maximum amount of money which can be spent to acquire a new customer. Breaking-even, at a mailing cost of $421.60/M, requires an initial response rate of 1 percent in order to recover acquisition costs over a five-year projection of customer activity.

PAR calculation should be done by product line and, under some conditions, even by source of new business. The calculation should be done at least annually, updating the assumptions used.

Enhanced PAR: The Lifetime Value of a Customer

PAR measures the value of *continuity selling*. Enhanced PAR lets the direct marketer measure the value of *cross selling* to a current customer. When *Time* magazine renews subscriptions of customers it has already acquired, it is practicing *continuity selling*. When it offers its present customers the opportunity to receive one or more of the *other* magazines it publishes, such as *People* or *Sports Illustrated*, it engages in *cross selling*. Each of these cross-selling opportunities opens the door to new continuity selling efforts. *All add to the value of a customer.*

By anticipating these future sales and projecting the lifetime value of a current customer, Enhanced PAR might help an organization decide to spend more on promotion to acquire new customers than those customers appear to be worth when considering only an initial sale.

This measurement is *Enhanced PAR*. It is calculated as the ratio of promotion cost to PAR Value, thus:

$$\text{PAR Ratio} = \frac{\text{Promotion Cost}}{\text{PAR Value}}$$

Thus, if the PAR ratio is 1.00, then new customers are being acquired at *exactly what they are worth over time* and still yield an assumed rate of return on investment.

If the PAR ratio is less than 1.00 (0.85, for example), *new customers are being acquired at less than their future value.*

If the PAR ratio is greater than 1.00 (1.40, for example), *more is being paid for the acquisition of customers than they will ever be worth* unless there is *another* source of revenue, such as *cross-selling* other products/services to that customer.

Figure 12.4 illustrates a product and source mix forecast which views customer acquisition as an investment. Five products to be offered to present customers and qualified prospects are identified by the letters A, B, C, D, and E. Anticipating that product offers to customers will generate a par ratio less than 1.00, the need in this composite forecast is to determine how much solicitation of prospects, at a PAR ratio greater than 1.00, can be accommodated.

The bottom-line objective, all products and all sources of orders combined, is a cumulative PAR ratio of 1.00—the point at which promotion costs—including inquiry follow-up and order fulfillment, but not cost-of-goods-sold or general administrative costs—exactly equal the value of the sales generated from these costs.

In Figure 12.4, costs related to acquisition of new orders (but not necessarily *new customers*) are shown left of the column titled "Mail/Space Volume/Circulation;" response results are shown to the right. Costs are related to the volume of promotion as well as the number of inquiries and orders to be processed.

Parenthetically, in the "# Inquiries" and "# Orders" columns are shown the response rates per thousand solicitations. Significant is the response rate from customers relative to that from prospects, which is 4:1 in the case of product A. Note, in the column headed "Order PAR Value" that each product has a unique PAR value, representing the continuity value of *that* sale, *but not cross sales, which are evaluated by PAR ratios.*

As anticipated, PAR ratios for all product orders from current customers—with the single exception of product C—are below 1.00. Product C's unfavorable PAR ratio of 1.03 indicates that this unprofitable effort should not be continued. To do so would not result in further amortization of the investment already made in that customer. The product should also be dropped from the line, since a product which cannot be sold profitably to a current customer likely has little appeal to those without a relationship with the organization.

Analyzing the PAR ratios of your products and order sources can help you enhance the profitability of your promotions. In this

FIGURE 12.4
Enhanced PAR calculated in a product/source mix.

Pro-duct	Source	Promotion $ Cost	Inquiry Fulfill $ Cost	Order Fulfill $ Cost	Total $ Cost	Mail/Space Volume/ Circulation	# Inquiries & (/M)	# Orders & (/M)	$ Sales Revenue	Order PAR Value	Total PAR Value	PAR Ratio	Cumulative PAR
A	Customers	$35,000		$40,000	$75,000	100,000		4,000(40)	$200,000	$24.38	$97,520	0.77	
	Mail Prospects	$87,500		$25,000	$112,500	250,000		2,500(10)	$125,000	$24.38	$60,950	1.85	
	Space Prospects	$30,000	$20,000	$20,000	$70,000	500,000	5,000(10)	2,000(4)	$100,000	$24.38	$48,600	1.44	
	Subtotal	$152,500	$20,000	$85,000	$257,500	850,000	5,000	8,500	$425,000	$24.38	$207,070	1.24	1.24
B	Customers	$35,000		$18,000	$53,000	100,000		3,600(36)	$108,000	$15.10	$54,360	0.97	
	Mail Prospects	$90,000		$31,500	$121,500	300,000		6,300(21)	$189,000	$15.10	$95,130	1.28	
	Space Prospects	$2,700	$12,960	$8,100	$23,760	270,000	3240(12)	1,620(6)	$48,600	$15.10	$24,462	0.97	
	Subtotal	$127,700	$12,960	$57,600	$198,260	670,000	3,240	11,520	$345,600	$15.10	$173,952	1.14	1.20
C	Customers	$90,000		$16,000	$106,000	200,000		2,000(10)	$240,000	$51.70	$103,400	1.03	1.16
D	Customers	$70,000		$16,800	$86,800	200,000		4,200(21)	$294,000	$29.88	$125,496	0.69	1.06
E	Customers	$10,000	(Stuffer)	$2,400	$12,400	200,000		2,400(12)	$216,000	$21.24	$50,976	0.24	1.00
	TOTAL	$450,200	$32,960	$177,800	$660,960	2,120,000	8,240	28,620	$1,520,600		$660,894		1.00

example, PAR ratios tell you that product B, which is only marginally appealing to current customers, may not be worth offering. On the other hand, it indicates that the low promotion cost of product E is as effective for creating profit as would be additional sales!

CASE STUDY

The Lifetime Value of a Customer

The lifetime value of a customer, recorded and authenticated in a database, was apparent in a *Wall Street Journal* article reporting the acquisition of Medco Containment Services—the "Wal-Mart of pills," according to the paper—by Merck and Company, the "Tiffany of drug makers." According to the story, Merck was buying Medco's technology and information database.

"Take a database detailing millions of drug prescriptions. Ask your computer which ones can be switched to your company's drugs. Employ pharmacists to suggest the switches to patients' doctors. That's the prescription for marketing success . . . "

This database-driven effort to use patient data to increase influence on the prescribing practices of physicians and to communicate directly with patients had an earlier episode. Back in the 1960s, an entrepreneurial pharmacist fresh out of school used a similar rationale to build his company, Pharmaceutical Services.

Founded by Charles "Chuck" Byrne, the company set its sights on the well-defined and growing senior citizen market. Older persons, it reasoned, would make ideal prescription drug customers. They had on-going and regular prescription needs. They sought convenience, did not need immediate delivery and required discount pricing.

What's more, research showed a direct correlation between drug prices and the clout of state pharmacy boards in regulating the advertising of such prices. Chuck began in a state which had strong advertising prohibitions, sending a pharmaceutical catalog featuring low prices through mail order so as to be beyond that state's regulatory arm.

Success was instantaneous. As the company's database grew, tens of thousands of *customer relationships* were built. The company's expertise and customer database were eventually acquired by another pharmaceutical manufacturer, which used it to launch direct-to-user operations.

Were the company's customers an asset? You bet! Applying the LTV concept to Pharmaceutical Services' customer list helped the new owner determine the market value of the enterprise before acquiring it. Since such an asset valuation reflects anticipated future performance, it can be a more accurate gauge of value than commonly used multiples of sales or profits.

Planning, Forecasting, Budgeting and Evaluating

Direct marketers, through measurement and accountability and the capturing of a customer database, plan for profit. Strategic planning is the essence of the direct marketing process from which evolves a system based on scientific decision-making. Planning looks at means versus ends, inputs versus outputs. Planning minimizes risks.

Profitable organizations engage in long-range planning for periods of two, three, five, and even 10 or more years. This kind of planning makes use of PAR and Enhanced PAR ratios to calculate the lifetime value of a newly-acquired customer. To update plans and weather inevitable changes, these companies turn to short-range forecasting, budgeting and evaluating for periods of three or six months or a year.

Forecasts and budgets are mathematical models formulated in terms of statistical probabilities, calculated to be correct a high percentage of the time and, on average, reasonably close to the actual occurrences. There are two major categories of forecasting methodology in common use. Build-up techniques derive total estimates from components of the forecast, such as accumulation of promotion offers into a total sales forecast. Relationship techniques derive estimates from correlation with market factors, such as demographics of a database. A build-up forecast is shown in the Workshop at the end of this chapter.

There are a variety of forecasting methodologies; some are highly sophisticated computer models. Classified according to the techniques employed, these methods include the following:

- *Judgment forecasts* are largely "seat-of-the-pants forecasts" based mainly on prior experience and insight. They often include no data; they are possibly most widely used.

- *Surveys of expectations* use polling methods to ask knowledgeable people about future events. These become more suitable when there is a historic reference point.

- *Time series or mechanical extrapolation* forecasts attempt to identify movements or trends that existed over past time periods, presuming that the future mirrors the past.

- *Moving averages* couple a series of averages that approximate a trend with exponential smoothing. This tends to cancel out the high and low values of the average over the time period.

- *Analytical forecasts* predict on the basis of information obtained from economic variables rather than simply the past history of the variable being projected. It is a popular causal method, using correlation and regression.

As meteorologists or economic forecasters do, direct marketers often *explain* after the fact rather than *predict*. *Planning* sets forth what is to be done; *evaluating* reviews what was accomplished. The evaluation process considers actual results in relation to forecast results and budgeted costs, and looks at the factors responsible for these results. A major objective of the evaluation is to identify misdirected effort.

A Forecast Model That Views Customers as Investments

Figure 12.5 shows a build-up forecast and budget with PAR enhancement. It demonstrates a five-year projection of lifetime customer value, its amortization and current market valuation.

This example, a start-up mail-order catalog, has no customer database at the outset. A "bounce-back" offer included with each shipment to a new customer is its first effort at cross-selling. As detailed in column (2), it acquires new customers beginning in 1996 with the mailing of a 12-page mini-catalog to selected response lists. It also employs publication space advertising to generate direct orders as well as to solicit inquiries for its catalog. This new-customer acquisition process is projected to continue for a five-year period, during which time the company builds its customer base—with each year's customer renewal rate shown in parentheses—and increases the size of its catalog.

Columns (3) through (8) detail the extent of each promotion effort—number and frequency of catalog mailings as well as space advertising expenditures—together with costs for each effort. Formulas are shown under each column heading.

Columns (9), (10), (12), (13), (14), and (15) detail predicted response and revenue, as well as the formulas for arriving at the numbers in these columns. Note that column (11) specifies an allowable order/inquiry cost (PAR), which increases year-to-year, and is applicable only to space advertising. This PAR value has been calculated independently and is also used to calculate break-even response rates for direct mail catalogs.

The constant 55 percent in column (16), applied to revenues in column (15), calculates the combined costs-of-goods-sold and general administrative costs in column (17). These costs are next added to promotion costs in column (8) to determine total production and promotion costs in column (18). Then, subtraction of total costs in column (18) from total revenues in column (15) provides, in column (19), a picture of customer investment.

PAR value, calculated independently, when multiplied times the number of *new* customers in column (13), is shown in column (20). PAR recovery, being the *positive* values in column (19), is shown in column (21). Finally, column (22) summarizes net cash investment, PAR and PAR recovery in order to reflect net customer value accumulation for each annual time period.

At the end of five years, as shown at the bottom of column (3), the firm projects that it will have 94,241 active customers. Their remaining lifetime value, shown at the bottom of column (22), is $784,875, an amount which can be considered to be the market valuation (goodwill) of the customer list. This amount is really understated, as customers acquired during the first year of operation are now fully amortized, although 2,457 of these are still active. Similarly, 5,608 customers remain from the second year with one year of amortization remaining. The resolution to this, which would reflect current market valuation more realistically, at a higher level, would be to extend the number of years for determination and amortization of PAR.

FIGURE 12.5

A build-up forecast/budget with PAR enhancements.

(1)	(2)	(3)	(4)	(5)	(6)	(7)	(8)	(9)	(10)	(11)	(12)
Year	Source/Lists	Est. Size of Source/List	Mailing Freq'cy	Total Mailed (3)×(4)	Mailing Cost/Pc	Space $ Adv/Inq	Promotion Cost Total (5)×(6)+(7)	Response Rate of Col. 5	Ttl Mail Response (5)×(9)	Ord/Inq Cost of Col. 7	Ttl Space Response (7)/(11)
1996	Customer (Bounce-back)	3,184	1	3,184	0.15		$478	10.00%	318		
	Response-12pg. Mini-catalog	100,000	1	100,000	0.53		$53,000	1.47%	1,470		
	Space Ads for Orders					$50,000	$50,000			$35.00	1,429
	Space Ads for Inquiries					$10,000	$10,000			$35.00	286
	TOTAL1996			103,184			$113,478		1,788		1,714
1997	Customer–1996 (90%)	2,866	5	14,329	0.85		$12,180	4.00%	573		
	Customer–1997 (50%)	3,452	2	6,904	0.85		$5,868	4.00%	276		
	Response–12pg. Mini-catalog	150,000	1	150,000	0.43		$64,500	1.19%	1,785		
	Response–36pg. Catalog	150,000	1	150,000	0.85		$127,500	2.36%	3,540		
	Space Ads for Orders					$50,000	$50,000			$38.00	1,316
	Space Ads for Inquiries					$10,000	$10,000			$38.00	263
	TOTAL-1997			321,233			$270,048		6,174		1,579
1998	Customer-1996(95%)	2,723	5	13,613	0.75		$10,210	4.00%	545		
	Customer-1997(90%)	6,214	5	31,068	0.75		$23,301	4.00%	1,243		
	Customer-1998(50%)	6,143	2	12,287	0.75		$9,215	4.00%	491		
	Response-36ppCatalog	450,000	1	450,000	0.75		$337,500	2.08%	9,360		
	Space Ads for Orders					$100,000	$100,000			$41.00	2,439
	Space Ads for Inquiries					$20,000	$20,000			$41.00	488
	TOTAL-1998			506,967			$500,226		11639		2,927
1999	Customer-1996(95%)	2,586	5	12,932	0.70		$9,053	4.00%	517		
	Customer-1997(95%)	5,903	5	29,514	0.70		$20,660	4.00%	1,181		
	Customer-1998(90%)	11,058	5	55,291	0.70		$38,704	4.00%	2,212		
	Customer-1999(50%)	13,974	2	27,947	0.70		$19,563	4.00%	1,118		
	Response-36 pg. Catalog	1,300,000	1	1,300,000	0.70		$910,000	1.94%	25,220		
	Space Ads for Orders					$100,000	$100,000			$44.00	2,273
	Space Ads for Inquiries					$20,000	$20,000			$44.00	455
	TOTAL-1999			1,425,685			$1,117,979		30,247		2,727
2000	Customer-1996(95%)	2,457	5	12,286	0.65		$7,986	4.00%	491		
	Customer-1997(95%)	5,608	5	28,039	0.65		$18,225	4.00%	1,122		
	Customer-1998(95%)	10,505	5	52,526	0.65		$34,142	4.00%	2,101		
	Customer-1999(90%)	25,153	5	125,763	0.65		$81,746	4.00%	5,031		
	Customer-2000(50%,	25,259	2	50,518	0.65		$32,837	4.00%	2,021		
	Response-36 pg. Catalog	2,650,000	1	2,650,000	0.65		$1,722,500	1.81%	47,965		
	Space Ads for Orders					$100,000	$100,000			$47.00	2,128
	Space Ads for Inquiries					$20,000	$20,000			$47.00	426
	TOTAL-2000	(Active Customers)		2,919,131			$2,017,435		58,730		2,553
GRAND TOTAL-1996–2000		94,241		5,276,201			$4,019,166		108,579		11,501

(13)	(14)	(15)	(16)	(17)	(18)	(19)	(20)	(21)	(22)
Total # Orders	Aver'g $Order (10)+(12)	Total $ Revenue (13)×(14)	C.O.G.S. +G/A	Fulfil't Costs (15)×(16)	Total Costs (8)+(17)	Customer Investment (15)−(18)	PAR: New Customers	PAR Recovery	Net Inv + PAR −PAR Recovery (19)+(20)−(21)
318	$12	$3,821	55.00%	$2,102	$2,579	$1,242		$1,242	
1,470	$55	$80,850	55.00%	$44,468	$97,468	($16,618)	$51,450		
1,429	$55	$78,571	55.00%	$43,214	$93,214	($14,643)	$50,000	·	
286	$55	$15,714	55.00%	$8,643	$18,643	($2,929)	$10,000		
3,503		$178,957	55.00%	$98,426	$211,904	($32,947)	$111,450	$81,773	($3,270)
573	$75	$42,988	55.00%	$23,643	$35,823	$7,165		$7,165	
276	$70	$19,331	55.00%	$10,632	$16,500	$2,831		$2,831	
1,785	$60	$107,100	55.00%	$58,905	$123,405	($16,305)	$67,830		
3,540	$65	$230,100	55.00%	$126,555	$254,055	($23,955)	$134,520		
1,316	$55	$72,368	55.00%	$39,803	$89,803	($17,434)	$50,000		
263	$55	$14,474	55.00%	$7,961	$17,961	($3,487)	$10,000		
7,753		$486,361	55.00%	$267,499	$537,547	($51,186)	$252,350	$200,814	$10,350
545	$85	$46,284	55.00%	$25,456	$35,666	$10,618		$10,618	
1,243	$80	$99,417	55..00%	$54,679	$77,980	$21,437		$21,437	
491	$75	$36,860	55.00%	$20,273	$29,488	$7,372		$7,372	
9,360	$70	$655,200	55.00%	$360,360	$697,860	($42,660)	$383,760		
2,439	$60	$146,341	55.00%	$80,488	$180,488	($34,146)	$100,000		
488	$60	$29,268	55.00%	$16,098	$36,098	($6,829)	$20,000		
14,566		$1,013,371	55.00%	$557,354	$1,057,579	($44,209)	$503,760	$413,291	$46,260
517	$90	$46.556	55.00%	$25,606	$34,658	$11,898		$11,898	
1,181	$85	$100,349	55.00%	$55,192	$75,852	$24,497		$24,497	
2,212	$80	$176,930	55.00%	$97,312	$136,015	$40,915		$40,915	
1,118	$80	$89,431	55.00%	$49,187	$68,750	$20,681		$20,681	
25,220	$75	$1,891,500	55.00%	$1,040,325	$1,950,325	($58,825)	$1,109,680		
2,273	$65	$147,727	55.00%	$81,250	$181.250	($33,523)	$100,000		
455	$65	$29,545	55.00%	$16,250	$36,250	($6,705)	$20,000		
32,975		$2,482,039	55.00%	$1,365,121	$2,483,101	($1,062)	$1,229,680	$1,028,938	$199,680
491	$95	$46,685	55.00%	$25,677	$33,662	$13,023		$13,023	
1,122	$90	$100,939	55.00%	$55,517	$73,742	$27,197		$27,197	
2,101	$85	$178,589	55.00%	$98,224	$132,366	$46,223		$46,223	
5,031	$85	$427,593	55.00%	$235,176	$316,922	$110,671		$110,671	
2,021	$80	$161,658	55.00%	$88,912	$121,749	$39,909		$39,909	
47,965	$80	$3,837,200	55.00%	$2,110,460	$3,832,960	$4,240	$2,254,355		
2,128	$70	$148,936	55.00%	$81,915	$181,915	($32,979)	$100,000		
426	$70	$29,787	55.00%	$16,383	$36,383	($6,596)	$20,000		
61,283		$4,931,388	55.00%	$2,712,264	$4,729,699	$201,689	$2,374,355	$2,044,189	$531,855
120,080		$9,092,116	55.00%	$5,000,664	$9,019,830	$72,286	$4,481,595	$3,769,006	$784,875

13

The Future of Direct Marketing

The future of direct marketing, like its present, lies in, first, the creation, and then, the cultivation of customers.

Customers can best be served by organizations that know the characteristics of their buyers as well as their buying patterns. An organization that knows about its customers, and their needs, will have no trouble providing products that fulfill them.

Tracking customer characteristics and transactions; then turning these into viable marketing information is, as we have shown in the prior 12 chapters, the job for a marketing database. Only a database can recognize such information, relating it to market segments that become the targets for effective promotion.

Today, there is a new direct marketing trend in the creation and cultivation of customers: *interactivity*. Emerging interactive media—such as personal computers, television/telephone hookups, and "smart cards"—provide greater convenience for customers, and enable organizations to gather more data about customers and their transactions. The so-called information highway is a direct marketing vision of the future even though a lot of it is here and now. However, no one yet knows how many, especially those not technically-oriented, will *accept* the concept.

This chapter looks at these three emerging interactive media: personal computers, television/telephone hookups, and the "smart card" as used by retailers. All three offer marketers the chance to create and cultivate closer relationships with customers using cutting-edge technology.

Personal Computers

The future is *now* insofar as personal computer applications for direct response are concerned. As many as one-third of about 100 million U.S. households have PCs. Some 90 percent of these are believed to have modems for telephone access to available on-line information services. Of those able to do so, about 4 million households—4 percent of all U.S. households—are subscribers.

The three major on-line services offering opportunities for direct marketers—CompuServe, Prodigy and America Online—provide consumer access to advertisers such as Lands' End, Barnes & Noble, Dreyfus, Ford and American Express. They also provide access to travel bookings, investment transactions, automobiles, computers, and a host of other consumer purchase possibilities.

Graphic presentations, once a major limitation of on-line shopping services, have been overcome with the introduction of the CompuServe CD multimedia combination of CD-ROM based information, applications, sound, graphics and video not heretofore available.

While the number of subscribers to on-line information services accessed through personal computers is growing by leaps and bounds, their usage is largely confined to communications, special-interest forums and a relative few of the up to 2000 service offerings, including electronic shopping. And since most on-line shopping is just that—shopping—the potential impact on the use of direct mail and catalogs by direct response advertisers appears to be negligible. In fact, because of the medium's presentation limitations as well as the drawback that "browsing" on-line is cumbersome, much response is of an inquiry nature. The medium is thus seen by many direct response advertisers to be mainly a means of qualifying a prospect, with market segments self-identifying.

This is especially true, at least at this stage, of the Internet, its World-Wide Web, and the proliferation of "home pages" therein. Even though these advertising pages are information-laden, it is still up to prospects to seek them out and then to self-identify as market segments. It is thus the prospect who must be pro-*active*, as well as technically inclined, in the search for benefits to fulfill needs—rather than the advertiser, whose objective it is to sell something through benefit-oriented, need-fulfilling offers targeted to database-qualified prospects. Some describe the Internet as a classified directory without order, lacking a Dewey Decimal System!

Television/Telephone Hookups

The history of interactive television/telephone hookups in the United States has been spotty, as experiment after experiment has been boldly launched and quietly withdrawn. More successful are the government-sponsored British Prestel and French Minitel interactive systems. These offer British and French citizens telephone directory listings, news, sports and weather; banking and bill paying; airplane, train, hotel and restaurant reservations; movie and theater listings; a variety of games; as well as opportunities for shopping.

TV home shopping is the single most successful instance of interactive television in the U.S., with the telephone serving as a response medium. Now a multi-billion-dollar enterprise, TV home-shopping merchandise credibility has been enhanced with designer names like Diane Von Furstenberg and Bill Blass and with trusted retailer names like Saks Fifth Avenue, Macy's, and Spiegel.

A weakness of television home shopping, however, not unlike direct-mail catalog shopping, is that customers have direct contact with neither the merchandise nor with the merchandiser. Clothes cannot be tried on, alternatives cannot be physically compared, and there is a time lag between purchase and delivery. Under these conditions, there is an element of trust and credibility which needs to be conveyed.

Counterbalancing these negatives are the convenience of remote TV home shopping, its 24-hour availability and its fit with today's lifestyles. Acceptance has been great but, like PC-oriented shopping, it is still largely experimental. It represents, as do mail-order catalogs, a minuscule fraction of all general merchandise sales.

Future success with already-successful TV home shopping will likely accrue mainly to those seeking to *create* new customers—as opposed to those seeking to *cultivate* those customers already acquired—with visual demonstrations of the types of products that are purchased on impulse, such as gem jewelry and specialty clothing. As yet, there is limited random access to specific products on demand by individuals. And, as with on-line PC shopping, prospects must self-identify from the mass TV audience.

Experiments employing "black box" interaction by individuals are being conducted by Time Warner, Southwestern Bell, Bell Atlantic, and other regional telephone companies. Interactive technology, both fiber-optic and wireless transmission, is advancing rapidly. It is conceivable that both database-defined prospects, as well as random access by present customers, are just around the corner. Cable TV home shopping, under these conditions, could one day become a video extension of direct mail, with customers using the telephone for response. Still to come, of course, is customer acceptance of the whole process.

The direct marketer's interest in the new electronic media is mainly in shopping, responding, ordering. Their watchword is *interactivity*. They are looking forward to letting customers respond instantly through their personal computers and television sets just as they are already doing with their telephones.

The Smart Card

Supermarket laser devices have long tabulated customer purchases to regulate store inventories. But a new wrinkle has been created by the smart card, which looks like (and can be made to act like) an ordinary credit card. Embedded in it, however, is a very small but powerful computer microchip that contains demographic and transaction data about the cardholder. Updated when it is inserted into a card reader during store checkout, the smart card can simultaneously record current transactions into the store's database and then even profile the characteristics of specific product purchasers.

For both the store and the providers of products sold in the supermarket, the database identifies customers and their preferences for their future direct-mail promotions. It also enables profiling of present customers so that prospects like them can be identified and solicited. Whereas supermarket advertisers have traditionally "broadcast" their messages to groups they think will come to their stores and buy their products, their new databases now allow them to "narrow cast" and target customers individually.

The smart card, too, enables stores to trigger promotions—geared to discount coupons, the amount of transaction or even purchaser demographics—through scanning at the point of sale. (This eliminates the current 98 percent "wasted" distribution of coupons.) Shoppers who become members of an affinity group, such as Procter & Gamble's Vision Value Club, a buyer reward program, establish a relationship with the store. The expansion of the database allows verification of purchases and can even lead to the calculation of the lifetime value of a customer.

Smart card usage by retailers seeking to reward affinity groups and build store traffic seems virtually unlimited. With smart cards and resulting databases, direct marketers will not have to guess who buys what. They will know.

An Aside: Is Direct Marketing Getting Too Personal?

Use of data culled from interactive customers and their transactions alarms privacy advocates. Will these privacy concerns impact on the future of direct marketing?

Such data can provide direct marketers with opportunities to mold their products to customer preferences. And, through the targeting of relevant messages and media to likely prospects, intrusive or "junk" advertising—that which is not relevant to the interests of the recipient—would be minimized.

As a reality, though, people do not always react favorably when they realize that what they buy triggers a flood of direct-mail promotions. A customer switching coffee brands might feel good about being thanked for that. Or, the customer might feel that his or her privacy has been invaded!

Privacy advocates also point to potential harm or injury to individuals as a result of data dissemination. A Presidential Privacy Commission, however, determined that receiving unwanted direct mail (that not relevant or qualified by a database), while a nuisance, did not itself constitute injury or an invasion of privacy, so long as there was not a breach of confidentiality.

Still, the "my mailbox is mine" argument should be heeded. It behooves the direct marketer to be responsible in both the acquisition and the use of data. Certainly not the least of the reasons for this is that it is inefficient, as well as costly, to send irrelevant direct mail advertising to those not interested. That is an important reason why more and more attention is being given to database market segmentation.

The Future of Direct Marketing . . . and YOU

This book has been about how *you* can create and cultivate customers . . . through providing benefits to them. Therein lies the future of direct marketing. Will the discipline of direct marketing be in your future, too?

Here, as we conclude, are the ingredients which differentiate, from traditional marketing, that marketing which is database-driven, targeted, and directed:

- customer/prospect databases

- a view of customers as assets with lifetime value

- ongoing relationships and affinity with customers

- databased market segmentation

- research and experimentation (testing)

- benefit-oriented direct-response promotion

- measurement of results and accountability for costs

Customers are the lifeblood of *any* organization . . . and the reason for it. Your enterprise thrives on customers. They are the source of your future revenues and your future profits.

But, who are *your* customers and prospective customers? *Where* are they? *How* are they created? *Why* are they cultivated? *What* is their lifetime value?

This book has provided the means for you to answer those questions. It has presented direct marketing as a philosophy of enterprise—an attitude, a belief, a process, a strategy, *a way of doing business that is customer-oriented*. Our goal has been to highlight that idea as we presented an overview of the scope and the power of a good many of the tools and the techniques of the discipline of direct marketing.

Their future use is now up to you!

Index

About the Author

Martin Baier is one of the leading direct marketers of contemporary business. His 40+ years' experience as a direct marketing professional culminated as Executive Vice President and a Director of the Old American Insurance Company. He developed and is currently Director of the Center for Direct Marketing Education and Research at the Henry W. Bloch School of Business, University of Missouri—Kansas City. In addition to his extensive activities in education, he consults with a broad variety of organizations now involved in or adopting the discipline of direct marketing.

Baier is author of *Elements of Direct Marketing* as well as numerous articles on the discipline. His landmark article "ZIP Code: New Tool for Marketers" (*Harvard Business Review*, Jan.–Feb. 1967) made a substantial contribution to the use of ZIP codes as a practical direct marketing tool. He also conducts direct marketing seminars throughout the United States as well as in Europe, Australia, New Zealand, and Asia.

Baier has been inducted into the Direct Marketing Association Hall of Fame. The Direct Marketing Educational Foundation presented him its Ed Mayer Award and the Direct Marketing Insurance Council named him Direct Marketing Insurance Executive of the Year. The Mail Advertising Service Association honored him with its Miles Kimball Award and the Ed Sisk Award for Direct Marketing Vision was bestowed by the Direct Marketing Association of Washington Educational Foundation. The John Caples Awards Board gave him its Andi Emerson Award for contribution of outstanding service to the direct marketing creative community.

TITLES OF INTEREST IN MARKETING, DIRECT MARKETING, AND SALES PROMOTION

For further information or a current catalog, write:
NTC Business Books
a division of NTC Publishing Group
4255 West Touhy Avenue
Lincolnwood, Illinois 60646–1975 U.S.A.